Riding THE black cockatoo

Riding THE black

john cockAtoo

danalis

ALLEN&UNWIN

Half the royalties from the sale of this book will go to the Wamba Wamba people, and will be used for cultural and environmental projects including the regeneration of Black Cockatoo habitat in the hope that the clan's totem animal can be successfully reintroduced to Wamba Wamba Country.

First published in 2009

Allen & Unwin
83 Alexander St
Crows Nest NSW 2065
Australia
Phone: (61 2) 8425 0100
Fax: (61 2) 9906 2218
Email: info@allenandunwin.com
Web: www.allenandunwin.com

Cataloguing-in-Publication details are available
from the National Library of Australia
www.librariesaustralia.nla.gov.au

Cover and text design by Stella and John Danalis / Peripheral Vision
Set in 11.5/18 pt Adobe Garamond Pro by Ruth Grüner

This book was printed in June 2010 at
McPherson's Printing Group
76 Nelson Street, Maryborough, Victoria 3465, Australia
www.mcphersonsprinting.com.au

3 5 7 9 10 8 6 4

Mixed Sources
Product group from well-managed
forests, and other controlled sources
www.fsc.org Cert no. SGS-COC-004121
© 1996 Forest Stewardship Council

The paper in this book is FSC certified.
FSC promotes environmentally responsible,
socially beneficial and economically viable
management of the world's forests.

This project has been assisted by the Australian Government through the
Australia Council for the Arts, its arts funding and advisory body.

Australian Government

Australia Council
for the Arts

To my mother and father,
who said 'Yes'

To Bianca and Ebony,
our future

Acknowledgements

Many hands carried Mary back to Country; your names,
tears and smiles are woven into these pages.

Writing this book has also been a part of Mary's
homecoming.

I humbly give my thanks to those who listened when
I needed to speak (sometimes about the unspeakable),
and encouraged me to stay at the keyboard (even when it
seemed like the most inhospitable place on the continent):
Judy Saunders, Boori Monty Pryor, Dr Max Quanchi,
Bryan Cook, Matt Cassidy, Steve Wyborn, Peter Creagh,
Alan Hamilton, Helen Belle Bnads, Dr Pee Tek Chan,
Stella Danalis, Ruth Grüner, Erica Wagner, Sarah Brenan.

WELCOME TO COUNTRY

Kurrumeruk the giant Murray cod, chased by the Yemurraki Dreamtime Rainbow Serpent, made the rivers, lakes and billabongs. Their tracks like our Ancestors are everywhere in Wamba Wamba Country. Burials form part of the tracks on our journeys to the afterlife.

Reconciliation means balancing the book of history. It is also about balancing out the injustices of our past with justice for the future so we can be at peace with our families, other people and the environment we live in. We take the good, the bad, ugly and beautiful in our histories. One ugly stain in shared history can become a glorious but profound point in our journey. Wiran, the black cockatoo with red feathers, has taken us for a flight of beauty and wonderment returning our lost Ancestor to Country.

Our Esteemed Ancestor has been returned by Warriors of a different ilk, but strong in common purpose. Strong people with strong minds know what is right and what is truth. Kindness and truth will open doors and break down barriers. Rivers of tears and a blue sky filled with *weyi* (song), *warrang-warrang* (corroboree) and joy, such is the wonder of the flight with the Wiran back to the *yemin-yemin* (burial ground) of the Wamba Wamba. Welcome to Country.

{ WYRKER MILLOO GARY MURRAY
WAMBA WAMBA NATION, MURRAY RIVER
APRIL 2009 }

FOREWORD

'Just a whitefella who's learned to listen, that's all,' says a Wik woman about John Danalis. Through listening comes this story about a skull called Mary, going home.

Some of it hurts. 'Like a kangaroo – iconic in the wild but troublesome in our paddock' is a reflection of me through the eyes of others. It puts a hurting on my heart so bad it makes the thought of death welcome. This is but one of the many ugly reflections in this amazing story that need to be read quietly inside then said out loud for all to hear.

But then there's the proud-to-be-a-blackfella words, 'You tell your old man how much the Wamba Wamba nation appreciates what he's doing. Tell him I'd like to buy him a beer. We really owe you for this one. We owe you big time.' Those words made the happy tears flow and mingle with the sad ones to make a pool of healing *kilta* (salt water) for my heart to swim in.

Selfless in its search for sanity of the soul, majestic and poetic, *Riding The Black Cockatoo* is a nation's journey through its growing pains of race and colour. We lie within the pages of black on white. We belong to this story and it belongs to us. Thank you, John, for having the courage to search and find ways that will make us all better. *Waddamullie wadjabimbi.* Thank you, welcome.

{ BOORI MONTY PRYOR

CO-AUTHOR OF *MAYBE TOMORROW*

MELBOURNE, MARCH 2009 }

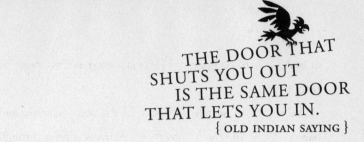

THE DOOR THAT
SHUTS YOU OUT
     IS THE SAME DOOR
THAT LETS YOU IN.
          { OLD INDIAN SAYING }

CHAPTER
ONE

Have you ever blurted something out in conversation, and a nanosecond later wished that you'd kept your trap shut? Well, that's the way my family secret came out – *blurt*! And once my secret was out, it just sat for all to see, like a bright blue jellyfish washed up by a king tide, stranded between the double glare of sun and sand, wishing it could wobble back into the ocean and glide inconspicuously once more among a billion other jellyfish secrets.

{ BRISBANE, LATE AUGUST–EARLY NOVEMBER 2005 }

This story goes way back, further back than any of us can imagine. But it became part of my family's dreaming just before I was born, 40 years ago. Like a distant storm flickering across the horizon, this story crept across the landscape patiently; it knew just when to announce itself, just when to hit. And when this story first began to rattle my windows I was a man – or perhaps just a boy – lost, still trying to find my path.

I'd tried lots of things in life, but nothing had stuck. I still hadn't found what I was meant to do, what I was supposed to be. I had a wife now, and two daughters who seemed to be blowing out birthday candles every other Sunday. I felt time was ebbing away. So I enrolled at university as a mature-age student and began a double degree in arts and education; I was – to everyone's great relief – soon to become a teacher. And it was there that I enrolled in a class called 'Indigenous Writing'. This class was a departure from the other subjects I'd been studying. I'd signed up for Indigenous Studies units in previous semesters but always chickened out at the last minute and changed to something 'safer'. I was unsettled by so many things surrounding Aboriginal

Australia; I felt ashamed of my own ignorance of their culture, I felt guilty and dirty over our theft of their country, and deep down, perhaps I was afraid that they possessed 'something' that if unleashed might upset the nice orderly nature of my white world. But I knew that I had to learn about Aboriginal culture and history – after all, I was studying to become a teacher, and an understanding of Australia's traditional owners seemed to me as important as anything I might teach in maths or science. So Indigenous Writing seemed a soft way in, and besides, the unit covered indigenous writing from all over the world, so it wouldn't be too confronting, too uncomfortable, *too* Aboriginal.

It was a small class of about fifteen, and the discussions meandered all over the place like a long, winding creek. Our lecturer was one of the sharpest people I had ever met, and the reading list she prepared read like the itinerary from an adventure holiday company: Inuit short stories, nineteenth-century anti-colonial novellas, Native American chants, desert poetry. It was like sliding into a warm bath with a stack of *National Geographic*s close at hand. Each week we got together for three hours to discuss the readings, setting off like well-fed, middle-class adventurers into the literary landscapes of 'the Other'. What a strange term, 'the Other'; to white people it conjures up images of figures lurking in the shadows, of big round eyes peeping out from the jungle edge, and in a strange way that is exactly what it refers to – people living outside the mainstream. Yet the term was originally coined by persons of colour (particularly coloured women) as a way of discussing the cultural dominance of mainstream society and the methods used to mark them as inferior. Over time the term has been embraced by other groups whose genetics, sexual orientation and lifestyles defy convention; the sort of people who baffle, shock, antagonise or titillate 'straight' society. But most commonly the term is still used by Indigenous people as a way of understanding how 'Otherness' has been forced upon them. 'The Other'; it was a buzz-phrase our little group deployed with uncomfortable regularity – as if any of us could ever truly understand what it meant to be shoved to the margins of society. We were all white, and most of us had similar world views; it was a caricature of a liberal arts class, in a safe, cosy environment. Of course, what the class really needed was half a dozen Indigenous people – or even one. Now *that* would have taken the discussions into some interesting territory! Besides our worldly lecturer, I don't think many of us in the room knew – really knew – a person of colour. In this class, the closest we came to 'the Other' was the occasional visit from an extremely angry young woman who felt the need to remind us regularly that she was 'queer' as well as thoroughly pissed off with the world. A heavy vapour trail of marijuana followed her into class and everywhere else she went on campus. But she seemed just as much of a cliché as we were. We all had the luxury to buy into whichever off-the-rack look we felt best projected our self-image: tree-hugger, tree-cutter, flag-waver, flag-burner – we all had the opportunity to choose. Cocooned in the cottonwool of white-bread suburbia, we were all quite comfortable and, I suspect, quite numb.

{ 14 SEPTEMBER 2005 }

After many weeks of sampling the outer reaches of Indigenous literature, the class finally got around to discussing 'the Australian situation'. We were sitting, as usual, around a long table sipping tea and coffee. It was very informal and relaxed, a class reminiscent of the 'good old days' when universities were places of inquiry and exploration rather than the biscuit-cutter conveyor belts of vocational training they tend to be now. I had scurried in late, but not very late; being a mature-age student I was generally punctual and studious (I'd been ejected from two campuses some 20 wild years ago and was determined not to blow it this time). As I took a seat, my ears pricked up; our lecturer was halfway through a confessional about her family's dark past. She recounted the brutal divide between the whites and Indigenous peoples of her childhood town in northern New South Wales. Aborigines fulfilling community service duties, usually as punishment for minor offences, were allotted the most humiliating and disgusting tasks by the community's police and menfolk. Often they were forced to work naked, sometimes before jeering onlookers with cameras. As she began to revisit the degradations and humiliations that these men and women had been subjected to, our lecturer's voice tapered off into an embarrassed silence, as if she'd already said too much, as if she'd already betrayed her bloodline. But she didn't need to go into detail; the weight that clawed at her face and shoulders finished the story and hinted at an upbringing burdened by unresolved memories. She would later share with me that she had kept closeted away, safe from her father's bigoted gaze, a photograph of her childhood tennis idol Evonne Goolagong.

Then came my announcement. Perhaps I said it to divert some of the attention away from the rattlings of my lecturer's family skeletons; I also suspect I said it partly out of the desire to go one better – mature-age students can be terrible know-alls and I was no exception.

'*Well*, I grew up with an Aboriginal skull on my mantelpiece.'

I said the words with a sort of worldly swagger, somehow expecting the announcement to impress my younger classmates. I might as well have unzipped my pants and flopped my penis onto the table – everyone turned and stared at me with a mixture of incredulousness, disgust and horror. My worldliness withered. There was silence; and in that seven-second eternity my childhood was teleported from the Polaroid feel-good fuzziness of the 1970s into the cold, hard glare of the year 2005.

And then came the chorus. 'You *what*? You have a *what* in your living room?'

'No, no, not *my* living room,' I backpedalled furiously; of course *I* was too enlightened to permit such a heinous display in my own home. 'It was on my family's mantelpiece, in the family home, where I grew up, and it's not as bad as you think, things were different back then . . .'

Now it was time for my voice to taper off. A different kind of silence filled the room. It was a silence accompanied by a collective unblinking stare, and I sat at its epicentre.

'Some—' my voice squeaked, 'someone – an uncle, actually – gave it to my father when I was a baby. I grew up with it, it was always there. Dad collected stuff, it just sat up on the wall unit with all his other bits and pieces; old stuff, rifles, wild boar tusks, deer antlers—'

The eyes grew wider.

'Guns?' asked one girl, almost tearfully. 'You mean this Aboriginal skull is displayed with guns, like a trophy?'

'And pigs' tusks?' added another.

'*Country people*, my family are country people, we grew up with guns. And it's not what it sounds like. Dad's a veterinarian, he's into stuff like that, he's even got two Siamese piglets floating preserved in a fish tank full of formaldehyde. The skull was a scientific curio, not a trophy.'

But it was too late; I had waded so far out into the gloop that every word I uttered just mired me deeper. I was up to my bottom lip in it. My beloved childhood home sounded like a cross between *Ripley's Believe It Or Not* and the trophy cave from *Wolf Creek*.

'Is it still there now?' asked the teary-eyed girl.

'No-o-o,' I answered with unconvincing reassurance. 'I asked Mum to put it away years ago, when she started babysitting my daughters. I didn't want them spooked out.'

'Spooked out'; what an understatement! Eventually the eyes turned away and the discussion moved on. And there I sat, utterly deflated. Over the years I could have filled a hot-air balloon with my bluster about equality, justice and the brotherhood of man; but here was this terrible truth – this secret shard – that brought my seemingly normal childhood and world view crashing back to terra firma.

I can't recall the first time I saw – I mean, *consciously recognised* – an Aboriginal person. Children, after all, don't naturally differentiate between people of colour, it is adults who hand out the labels, generation after generation. 'Australian Aborigine' sounds so anthropological, almost zoological – like 'Australian marsupial'. Yet in a strange way that was how I was brought up to see Indigenous Australians, as some sort of museum exhibit; an oddity that sat somewhere on the evolutionary scale between Og the Caveman and a brave white fellow in a pith helmet called Rupert. I was taught that it was acceptable to marvel at the Aborigine in his natural setting – preferably in the most distant corner of a far-flung desert, where he could launch boomerangs or sit in the shade of a brigalow tree to his heart's content. We admired his hardiness and his healthy, gleaming, 'Yes, boss' smile as he looked up to the camera – as long as he stayed on the far side of the horizon. Like the kangaroo – iconic in the wild but troublesome in *our* paddock – Aboriginal contact tended to upset our idea of the order of things. Indigenous people disturbed the neat fencelines of our logic; they messed with our empirical minds. For *their* collective mind seemed like a mysterious storehouse stacked high with what the modern world considered superstitious mumbo-jumbo and redundant knowledge. Only now are we awakening to an understanding that this 60 000-year-old storehouse holds answers to questions we have just begun to ask. The custodians of this storehouse possessed a playful ability to live in the moment that both baffled and annoyed the hell out of us. But of course our biggest bugbear was the colour of their skin.

Black. The negative images embedded in our language go back centuries; black is the night, black is my soul, burnt black, eyes black with rage, black heart. To a white boy growing up in the safe, suburban 1970s, 'black' conjured up the beating native war drums of Saturday-afternoon Tarzan movies. It meant cannibal cooking pots, violated white missionary women, and spears thrust deep into the unsuspecting backs of noble explorers. It meant voodoo, shrunken heads, witchdoctors and inexhaustible armies of fanatical Zulu warriors. As a small child I was chased down the jungle tracks of my imagination by every black cliché imaginable; a Negroid Frankenstein stitched together from Hollywood and *Boy's Own Annuals*. African, Caribbean, Islander, Australian; they were all tarred with the same evil brush. Black was black, and even in a suit or a doctor's gown, I was warned, a spear-chucker lurked just below the surface. As I type these recollections I cringe at how monstrously offensive such stereotypes are. In fact, I can't believe I'm writing this at all. Part of me wants to skip to the next chapter; it would be so much easier for all of us. But if this story is going to make any sense, it has to include everything; I need you, my reader, to peek into the freight cars full of baggage I've been dragging behind me all these years. Of course, none of this will be big news to Indigenous folk!

As a child, I viewed Black Australia through the same smudged lens that I imagine a lot of other people looked through. It was a lens that allowed us a one-way intimacy, like those one-way windows in police line-up rooms; we gawked and scrutinised without getting up close. And if we didn't like what we saw, or if what we saw made us uncomfortable, we could turn away, turn the page, switch the channel or change the subject. Not that the subject of Black Australia came up that often. To show too much interest in Aboriginal affairs aroused suspicion; to speak in their defence amounted to betrayal. Australians then didn't much like do-gooders; they seemed to somehow threaten our way of life, our collective values and our right to a good time. But if do-gooders were tolerated, 'Abo-lovers' were despised. We appropriated the term 'Nigger-lover' from the

Americans and re-jigged it to suit our language. And like the Americans, we used the term to keep 'our own kind' in line – just as a bitch nips at its young pups for straying too far from the litter. That's how it was when I grew up.

It's hard to imagine just how straitjacketed by conformity most Australians were only three or four decades ago. Take beer, for instance. In the 1970s, 99 per cent of Queensland beer drinkers drank Fourex – and full strength at that. Walking into a party or barbecue with another brand like Foster's or Carlton (there wasn't much to choose from back then) immediately branded you an outsider. If you were visiting from overseas or had recently migrated from the southern states it was forgivable, you were let off with a mild ribbing. But if you were a local and actually *preferred* the taste of that southern swill to Fourex, you were immediately branded by the phalanx of men huddled around the barbecue as someone of questionable social standing – an eccentric, an academic or a poofter, and certainly not one to be trusted with the ladies. That was beer! It seems unbelievable now. So just imagine what it was like to buck the social norms governing race relations in this country. Of course there were brave souls who did, but I never met one.

When the subject of Aboriginal Australia came up during my childhood, which was rarely, it was usually in the form of third-hand stories or jokes. The stories went like this: 'A mate of my cousin's works somewhere out west, and he swears that this is true; when the blackfellas run out of petrol they push their government-funded Toyotas off the side of the track and set fire to them – too lazy or too stupid to refill 'em. They just wait until they get another government vehicle and do the same thing all over again. Useless bastards, all of 'em, and we're footin' the bill.'

The other men around the barbecue, bar or lunch-room would all shake their heads in disgust and utter statements like 'Useless black pricks'.

Then, without fail, one of the more sensitive souls in the group would roll out this chestnut: 'Trouble is, the poor bastards are cavemen. I hate to say this, but they would've been better off if we'd wiped 'em all out.'

I heard that statement many times over the years and I could never help but wonder, 'Hang on, just how could an extinct race be *better off*?'

But of course I never asked the question out loud.

Then there were the jokes; there seemed to be an inexhaustible supply of Abo jokes doing the rounds of the schoolyards and campfires of my youth. We often brought these gags from home; and the fact that Uncle Bazza had told them around the table at Sunday lunch seemed to legitimise their craven humour. Deep down I had an inkling that something was amiss and my stomach often twisted in guilty discomfort, but it was always easier to laugh along. These jokes were never really funny and they connected with the mean streak that lurks within us all, the mean streak that left unchecked can spread like a toxic bloom. There was one particular joke that stepped beyond meanness. This joke began circulating during the 1980s Royal Commission into Aboriginal Deaths in Custody. This was a major inquiry into the disproportionate number of Aboriginal men who were committing suicide or dying while in police watch-houses and prisons. I found this joke so disturbing that every time I heard it, the seconds seemed to slow down as I waited for an adult – anyone – to say, 'Now listen here, that's not funny! Those dead men have grieving mothers.' But no one said a thing, least of all me. Another memory, another shard for my hot-air balloon.

The joke ran like this:

What do you call three blackfellas in a prison cell?
A mobile.

CHAPTER
TWO

{ 18 SEPTEMBER 2005 }

A few days after my big announcement to the class, I called into my parents' house to feed the cat; they had gone away for the weekend. I hadn't been sleeping well; I'd lain awake all night obsessing about the skull and the girl in my class – her unbelieving eyes. As I stood at the kitchen sink replenishing the cat's water bowl, I decided to look for Mary. That was the name my father had given to the skull when it was handed to him 40 years ago. Years later, a medical specialist told Dad that the cranium actually belonged to a male, but the female name stuck. The specialist also informed Dad that the 'specimen' had most likely died from syphilis. Syphilis, or 'the pox' as it was called in the days when it was common and highly feared, is a sexually transmitted disease that if left untreated eats away the organs, including the brain, and literally rots the skull from the inside out, causing agonising pain, madness and then death. This disease was just one of many that English soldiers, sailors, convicts and settlers brought to Australia. Before contact, the Indigenous population was largely free of influenza, tuberculosis, whooping cough, measles and most sexually transmitted diseases. Aboriginal people had no immunity to these alien diseases, and when they spread the local population perished – not just in ones or twos, but often by the community.

'See these cracks and lesions on the temple,' my father used to explain knowingly to curious visitors, 'that is where the syphilis ate away at the skull. The poor wretch would have been quite insane when he died.'

I started to poke around the mantelpiece, where Mary had always sat. When Mum and Dad started babysitting my first daughter, Bianca, I had quietly asked Mum to put Mary out of sight. She understood. It was easier approaching Mum on such a delicate matter; Dad would have responded with one of his looks, the kind that suggested in no uncertain terms that I'd gone soft in the head.

The 'mantelpiece' was really a 1960s wall unit that took up an entire wall. The bottom consisted of cupboards containing Mum's good dinner set and boxed pewter doodads – things given at births and christenings, things put aside for special occasions that never actually saw the light of day; the sorts of things that when you open them release the scent of four-decades-old air. There were photo albums here, and an enormous case of slides, a cantankerous old slide projector and a rolled-up, yellowed screen that had long forgotten what it was to be flat. The centremost cupboard had once snugly housed the television set; now, in this age of widescreen plasma, it housed Dad's collection of football videotapes. Above the bottom cupboard level was a sort of buffet area on which sat my parents' new TV, their stereo gear and record collection; and above that were two levels of shelves for books, framed photographs and prized pieces from Dad's collection of curios.

Dad had been a bush vet, a vocation which generously fed his appetite for collecting. Over the decades his profession had taken him into hundreds of the nation's farmyards, outbuildings and machinery sheds. Amid the smell of bagged animal feed, fertiliser, diesel oil and cracked leather, his magpie eye would scan the gloom for dust-caked treasure hanging from rafters or half concealed beneath ancient tarpaulins. Over the years Dad had amassed a mind-boggling haul. He had scores of antique bottles on display around the house and many more in crates. There were convict-made bricks with the makers' thumbprints still clearly visible; there were rusted handshears gleaned from shearing-shed walls; tobacco tins, branding irons, dingo traps, rabbit traps, and snakeskins as long as beds. He'd collected interesting pieces of stone kicked up in paddocks and cattleyards: thunder-eggs, chunks of petrified wood, clusters of quartz, even a baby-head-sized lump of coal. He carted home horse-driven ploughs and pre-Federation hand tools, a grinding stone the size of a car wheel, blown-out Model-T Ford radiators, kerosene-powered refrigerators, and rusted-out milk urns. There was *so* much stuff. He had a double-ended timbercutter's saw the length of a small car which was thoughtfully displayed next to the metre-long, toothy-edged nose of a sawfish (not many families had one of those!). But it wasn't all blokey stuff, he also had an eye for the delicate: fob and pocket watches, an exquisite pair of round-rimmed tortoiseshell glasses that I liked to imagine once belonged to a Chinese spice trader, miniature scales for measuring gold dust, snuffboxes of carved bone, old pearl brooches and pins, silver matchbox holders and ladies' pocket mirrors. At the height of my father's mania, it was not unusual to wake up and find a horse-drawn buggy (without the horse) that he had lugged home from the bush and reassembled overnight in the front yard.

Dad was a keen sportsman too, and there was a constantly fluctuating collection of rifles, guns and muskets. There were bayonets, a wickedly sharp Gurkha fighting knife, and an intricately inlaid samurai sword. There were the brass casings of artillery shells, and assorted bullets of every size. There were deer antlers, and the razor-sharp tusks from wild boar that he had dispatched on regular hunting trips.

Show-and-tell days at school were never a challenge; my brother and I would just grab something – anything – from around the house. Even if we didn't know what the object actually was, we could always make up a good story. My favourite was an old grinding iron from a flour mill; it was about the size of a cricket ball, black and mottled, and to the untrained eye looked like a small cannonball. I remember regaling my classmates with stories of how it had been used by Captain Cook's crew to disperse 'troublesome natives' as they were preparing to land their longboats on the beach of Fraser Island. I told them my father had been on a fishing trip when it was washed up by a wave at his feet – all three kilos of it! No one ever bothered to ask how we knew the history of this great lump of iron; my classmates – especially the boys – were too busy turning the Fraser Island Cannonball over in their hands with the silent reverence that boys bestow on implements that kill and maim.

Dad's collection could be divided into three broad categories. First there was the outside stuff – artefacts that were either too large to fit in the house or so grimy and dilapidated that they couldn't get past Mum. Then there was the downstairs stuff that filled drawers and boxes in the garage and lined the walls of the pool room. Third, there was the upstairs collection, the bits deemed special enough to live with us: the lamps, the vases, the pottery pieces, the shiny brass things, and of course Mary on the shelf above the record player. Mary sat in for every record change of my childhood. From the swinging sounds of Herb Alpert and the Tijuana Brass in the 1960s to Nirvana's bellowing-at-the-moon through the 1990s, four decades of middle-class white music reverberated though Mary. I sometimes wonder what his spirit would have thought of it all, especially on nights when the windows rattled to Mum and Dad's favourite, the thunderous organ prelude to *Phantom of the Opera*. It's a wonder that the combined sonic assault of Andrew Lloyd Webber and modern speaker technology hadn't reduced Mary to dust, or at the very least vibrated his teeth from their sockets.

I worked my way through the cupboards with a detective's touch, sneaky fingers feeling around corners, behind picnic baskets and over little boxes tied up with string. As a child, I had an almost paranormal knack for unearthing our gifts weeks before birthdays and Christmas. I peeked behind framed family photos up on the higher shelves, making sure that everything was put back just so. I said hello to my grandmamma, 20 years gone, and she smiled back at me through the dust-speckled glass from her beloved garden. In that photo, wild grey hair that she could never be bothered with blew in an eternal breeze and a green cardigan stretched across her abundant frame. How I loved her.

I abandoned the wall unit and wandered down the hall to my old bedroom. It's a bit of a junkroom now, a holding pen for things my mother is trying to get out of the house, and things my father is trying to hang onto. My old bedroom, once made wall-less by imagination; I saw again the Himalayan base camp on top of my wardrobe where I would sit amid clouds with my survival rations of Vegemite sandwiches. I saw again the endless shark-filled ocean over which my creaky bed rolled; I saw again the virgin, pea-green, shag-pile Amazonian forest over which my model planes floated. I looked through the window, seeking out familiar sights; the fire station tower where the hoses still hung like spaghetti strands dripping themselves dry; across the street, the young married woman's bathroom window on which I had trained my binoculars at 7.15 each night for one wonderful year – where was she now? The bedroom walls began to close in – too many memories for such a tiny room.

I drifted around downstairs, eyes and fingers flitting through the pool room, the workshop, my brother's old bedroom stacked high with things that had not yet made the skip or the local auction centre. The auction centre! In a recent effort to de-clutter the house and to appease my mother, Dad had been taking stuff there by the ute-load . . . Surely not! They wouldn't accept a human skull, would they?

I went back into the lounge room and flopped into my father's lounge chair. It sat dead square in front of the wall unit; the best seat in the house for watching the telly. The cat glided between my legs, her appreciative purring the only sound as I wondered out loud, 'Where? *Where* could Mary be?'

In the distance a rubbish truck emptied wheelie bins in quick, cacophonous crashes of falling beer bottles and the dull thuds of rubbish bags. 'Oh god, not the wheelie bin, not that!' I imagined Mary lost forever in landfill, entombed in maggoty meat scraps, festering nappies and all the never-to-break-down plastic refuse that makes up twenty-first-century waste.

Family homes are like time machines; just the hint of an odour, the groan of a loose floorboard, the slant of morning sunshine through half-opened drapes can peel away years, even decades. I gazed down at the lounge-room floor and pictured my brother and me sprawled out on the carpet with pillows and blankets watching Saturday-morning TV. I drifted back even further, remembering Neil Armstrong's first step into moon dust; I remember the big fuss being made by the adults in the room and being told it was too bad that I wouldn't remember the moment. I was three years old and I remember it all. The whole world was space-crazy; perhaps that is why we were disdainful of Indigenous culture. Now we were hurtling through space, did we see boomerangs as an embarrassing reminder of our origins?

I grew up on a cultural combo of American and Japanese cartoons and Australian children's television drama. All the shows were great, but there was *one* show that every young kid rushed home from school for: *Skippy the Bush Kangaroo*, the hit children's afternoon television show from the mid-1960s to the mid-1970s. Skippy was the star of the show, but it was his partner in adventure, the gumleaf-blowing Sonny Hammond, that every little boy wanted to be. Sonny had the biggest back yard in Australia; the fictional Waratah National Park where he lived a Boy's Own life with his park-ranger father Matt Hammond, brother Mark, and the daring chopper pilot Jerry. Sonny wasn't even encumbered with a mother telling him to be home for dinner or rousing on him for messing up his signature red-and-white-striped shirt. Together Sonny and Skippy hopped and clambered through bushland, rafted across shark-filled inlets, and roamed through hidden valleys and into the imagination of many an Australian boy and girl. And it was in one of these hidden valleys that Sonny and Skippy stumbled upon Tara.

Tara looked as though he'd just jumped off the two-dollar coin. He was as black as black could be, with wiry white hair and a sinewy grace. There was a lovely economy to his movements and he spoke like a sage. He was the cliché native Australian, but he was a magnificent cliché all the same. Tara was the last of a clan that had been relocated from its tribal country decades before. When Sonny and Skippy stumbled into the Hidden Valley – accessible only through a spooky secret cave – they found Tara living as his ancestors had, in a simple humpy high on an escarpment from where he could survey the valley below; a valley that provided sustenance for his belly and his spirit. Tara's only concession to the twentieth century was a discreet pair of red underpants – it was a children's show after all. Sonny was besotted with Tara – and what ten-year-old wouldn't be? The pair threw boomerangs, hunted for bush tucker and chilled out on the escarpment as fluffy white clouds rolled overhead. One lazy afternoon as the two sat enjoying the silence, Sonny turned to his friend. 'You're like Skippy, Tara, happy and free. You do whatever you please. I bet there are a lot of people that would like to change places with you.'

The boy had a point – Tara's life did have a certain Robinson Crusoe appeal to it – but in reality Sonny's words were no more than a scriptwriter's pipedream. In the 1970s, as now, you would have been hard pressed to find too many White Australians willing to trade places with an Aboriginal person.

No episode of *Skippy* was complete without nail-biting drama, and halfway into the show it came from the sky. On a routine air patrol over the park, Jerry decided to look for Sonny in the Hidden Valley. As the helicopter blades thrashed at the air over Tara's campsite, the terrified elder became convinced that the horrendous hovering noisemaker was the 'spirit of death'. Tara ordered his young friend to leave the valley so that he could prepare to join his ancestors. 'Time for

Tara to die, leave this place of death.'

'Please, Tara, please don't die. We're not going to let you die,' Sonny pleaded, tears streaming down his freckled cheeks.

That afternoon, little kids all around Australia repeated Sonny's words like a mantra: 'Please, Tara, please don't die!'

And then, something *truly* terrible happened. Three little words crawled across the screen: 'To be continued . . .'

The Tara episode was just too big to fit neatly into a half-hour slot, and had been split into two halves. The words *To be continued* could be a devastating thing for a child of seven. That evening as I slurped milk from my Skippy mug and picked listlessly at the dinner on my Skippy plate, I stared blankly into the lime-green geometric kitchen wallpaper, pondering Tara's fate. As I lay in bed under the subtropical sky, my sweaty head tossed and turned on my Skippy pillowcase. The next day, there was a palpable sense of tension in the schoolyard. By four o'clock, the streets, playgrounds and back yards that usually resonated to the sounds of bicycle bells and cricket bat thwacks fell silent. Every little Australian knew that in Aboriginal culture 'pointing the bone' was an act of sorcery, a curse that brought about certain death. I'm sure my little brother wasn't the only bullied child to point a half-gnawed chop bone at an annoying older sibling and announce, 'That's it, you're dead.' But this was the real deal; Tara had effectively pointed the bone at himself and was halfway back to the Dreamtime. Only Sonny and Skippy could save him. It was absolutely gripping stuff, and we were all as gripped as gripped could be!

As the sun slowly set on Tara's life, Sonny desperately rummaged through the old man's few belongings and discovered a medal and citation for bravery. As a younger man, Tara had heroically saved a small boy from drowning, and that small boy had grown up to become a powerful dignitary. Upon hearing of Tara's plight, the well-heeled dignitary organised the airlift of a songman and a full troupe of dancers from Tara's far-flung Akara tribe to be by their fading tribesman's side. *Skippy the Bush Kangaroo* had never seen anything like it, and neither had we; a dozen painted-up full-blood Aborigines (in underpants) dancing in jerky supernatural movements. The continual drone of the didgeridoo and the clack-clack of clapsticks echoed throughout the Hidden Valley and through Australian lounge rooms from coast to coast. The ceremony ran uninterrupted for ten mesmerising minutes. The dancers jerked slowly around an unconscious Tara, tension building, until at last his eyes flickered open and he slowly rose, joining his tribesmen in their otherworldly dance. And so the ending was a happy one; Tara was saved and allowed to stay on in the park, and Australian children were treated to an extended encounter – however artificial – with Indigenous Australia. At the end of the show, after some well-intentioned dialogue about black and white having much to learn from each other, Tara pronounced that 'Tara has many friends.'

I'm sure that at that moment every child watching wanted a friend just like Tara; a friend to reveal to them the mysterious secrets of the country in which they lived. For most of us, however, there would be no Tara to show us the ropes, and besides, we would soon be too distracted growing up into busy white Australians to remember or care.

I returned from my memories, rose and opened the centre TV cupboard of the wall unit again. Inside, stacked high, were videotape towers of AFL football games – Essendon games mostly, and a smattering of finals matches. I poked my head into the cupboard for a closer look. As my nostrils registered the faint, lingering whiff of burnt-out Rank Arena valves, I accidentally brought down a teetering pile of videos. There he was, Mary, upside-down in the far back corner of the TV cupboard – how uncomfortable he looked. Gently taking the skull from the cupboard, I returned to my father's chair. I put him to my nose and inhaled (don't be shocked, we were old friends). My grown-up fingers reconnected with him, tracing the little cracks that ran like the rivers of a faded atlas. The temple – the area known in spirituality as the third eye – was corroded by the syphilis that would have gnawed away at Mary's sanity and spirit.

Placing two fingers into the base of the skull, I recalled how once my entire hand and wrist could fit inside this space; I remembered the way I once wiggled my index and pinkie fingers through the eye sockets like graveyard worms. My fingers glided over the dry interior; once there was fluid here, and a brain floating in a continuous synaptic lightning storm that swept this way and that over a landscape of consciousness. Hunger and contentment, triumph and disappointment, wonder and awareness, every thought and feeling; they had all resided there in that cavity. My fingers felt like a stranger's legs, tiptoeing about in a long-deserted house, wondering at the private dramas and dreams which had once played out inside.

How yellow it had gone. Dad used to lacquer the skull every so often to prevent the bone from crumbling away into chalk and, I suspect, because he enjoyed lacquering things. After Mary was given to him, he had glued the lower jaw into position with Araldite and fixed a matchbox-sized block of wood to the base of the skull to prevent it from tipping over backwards. The teeth – except for one at the front – were all accounted for and in remarkably good condition – testimony, no doubt, to a cola- and chip-free diet. There had been the odd occasion in the 40 years that Mary sat on the shelf, firm-jawed and resolute, when some joker – usually when my parents were hosting a party – had placed a cigarette into the gap left by the missing tooth. And there were a few occasions when my younger brother Guy and I would test the nerves of the neighbourhood kids by placing a small pocket torch inside Mary so that the eye cavities and the slight gaps between his teeth glowed with an otherworldly radiance. We had the ultimate jack-o'-lantern. Although we sometimes revelled in the macabre weirdness of living with a skull on the mantelpiece, we always handled Mary with care. Apart from the occasional cigarette, Mary was never mocked or ridiculed; he became part of our landscape. It seemed no different to having my grandmother's ashes on display next to my grandfather's false teeth and a dried-up block of his favourite chewing tobacco (which we did!). There was a twisted yet sweet form of suburban ancestor worship going on in our house, and in a weird way Mary had come along for the ride.

My rational self knew the skull was as empty as the abandoned shell of a hermit crab, yet my heart told me otherwise; I felt *something*, but whatever it was, the harder I tried to see it – to understand it – the further I pushed it away; it was as elusive as mist. I tried to send some positive thoughts to the bones in my lap, something profound, but it was a strain to think; I wondered if I was losing my mind, yet at the same time there was a rare and unfamiliar calmness about my thoughts suggesting I ride this ripple that seemed to swell with each passing moment. I put Mary back with the tapes – the right way up this time – and jiggled him about a little to make him more comfortable. Then the words came, three simple words: 'You're going home.'

CHAPTER
THREE

{ 19 SEPTEMBER 2005 }

Missed my morning lecture, again. Interpersonal Relationships 101, not exactly the most captivating of subjects, but it would take me twelve credit points closer to a degree I should have finished years ago. And besides, I'd decided that some of my own interpersonal relationship skills could do with a bit of an overhaul. In a sunny corner of the library I scanned the weekend papers before attempting the set readings from my textbook. Mary was never far from my thoughts and there was a notion forming in the back of my brain that perhaps I could approach the University for help.

At lunchtime, I spied Craig from the Oodgeroo Unit (the campus Indigenous education and support department). He was eating lunch, alone.

'Do it, man, just walk over there and do it,' I told myself.

Craig had been a guest lecturer last semester in one of my Community Studies units, so I felt as though I knew him a little. He had opened his lecture with a simple yet powerful little 'party trick'; he fished all the loose change from his pocket and laid the coins out in a neat line on the overhead projector, from the lowest denomination to the highest.

'Five-cent piece – the echidna,' he began. 'Ten-cent piece – the lyrebird; twenty-cent piece – the platypus; one-dollar coin – a mob of kangaroos; two-dollar coin – a blackfella.'

He paused for a moment, waiting for the penny to drop; it hadn't yet for me.

'That fella there is supposed to represent Indigenous Australia,' he said, pointing to the chiselled face of the black bushman on the coin. It was the sort of iconic cliché that is part of the Australian lexicon; an Aborigine frozen for a moment as he stares out from some faraway escarpment at his vanishing country. It's the same blackfella who appears on old prints, postcards and biscuit tins; he balances on one sinewy leg, leaning ever so slightly on a brace of spears. It's an image that acknowledges a certain wisdom and grace, yet has a loneliness about it suggesting this fellow – like Tara – is the last of his tribe.

'And look at this, here's an extra little insult.' He pointed the tip of his pen to a grasstree cast into the background of the coin. 'You know what those are called, don't you?'

Half the students in the lecture theatre mouthed the word 'Blackboy'.

Craig nodded. He looked pleased that he'd made his point, yet there was a hint of weary bitterness simmering just below.

'You see, this is where we fit into the white scheme of things, as fauna, part of the animal kingdom, part of the landscape.'

One brave soul raised his hand and reminded the lecturer that the fifty-cent piece could have any number of things on it, like Captain Cook, or Charles and Diana. Craig laughed as if he'd expected the comment, 'Ah, the fifty-cent piece, that's the wild card, it can have anything on it, but it's usually a famous whitefella.'

Then he asked, 'How would you like to see a generic white person on that coin? Can you imagine where you would even start? You're all so different, you've all got different stories. Well, it's the same with us.'

Now I wandered across the grey expanse of concrete to where Craig sat outside the bustling University refectory. I asked if I could join him. He looked up, a little surprised, not sure if he should recognise me or not.

'Sure,' he answered, 'but I'm heading back to the office in a sec.'

As I explained that I needed to talk to him about 'something sensitive', I realised that this was the very first Indigenous Australian I'd ever spoken to one-on-one. Then without missing a beat I announced that my family had had one of his kin on display in the family lounge room for 40 years. I might as well have just walked up to the man and punched him in the guts. He recoiled in his seat as pain and disbelief tore across his face. Again, the seconds groaned – taut, dislocated from the clock time that marched on about us. Craig recovered, pushed away the last remnants of his sweet-and-sour pork, and rose to his feet.

'You'd better come with me,' he said; there was

just the hint of an order in his tone. Not a word was exchanged as he led me to the Oodgeroo Unit, named after the famous Aboriginal poet and activist Oodgeroo Noonuccal.

As we entered the office I immediately felt like an outsider, a whitefella in a blackfella place. It wasn't threatening, but the very atmosphere felt different. If you have ever visited a foreign consular office you'll know the feeling I'm trying to describe, it's as if a tiny piece of one country has been transplanted into another, and that's what this was like, a portal into Indigenous Australia. Black faces looked down from posters, and dot paintings, flags and panoramic photographs of wild Australia adorned the walls; there was familiarity about much of what I saw, yet at the same time everything was imbued with a different meaning. It was as if I'd stumbled into a parallel universe and now I was the foreigner!

Craig led me through to his office. A poster of the boxer and football star Anthony Mundine glared at me as though he was about to jump from the photograph and jab my soft white nose repeatedly! I stiffened for a moment, and then understood how this fighter, whom I'd always dismissed as an angry egomaniac with a super-sized chip on his shoulder, could be an inspiration to many of his people. Why had I looked down so disapprovingly upon black anger? Why was it acceptable for whites to get angry, but not black people? I looked around the room for a softer visual to grab hold of and my eyes settled on a photograph of Craig's wife and kids. There were photos of the land too – beautiful photos of rippling red soil and purple skies, the steamy, still breath of wetlands, and eternally teetering mega-boulders. I breathed easily again, comforted by these things that bind us.

Craig asked me about the skull and I let my story unfold. Every so often I paused and he shook his head rapidly as if to make sure his ears were not playing tricks on him. He looked at me with equal measures of sternness and sadness. 'It has *got* to go back, there's no question about it. You'll just have to convince your old man to give it up. It has to go back.'

At first I was a bit shocked; I wasn't exactly expecting a pat on the back, but I hadn't anticipated such grave (no pun intended!) seriousness either. I'd just presumed that there was some *place*, some *department* to send 'lost skulls' to and that was the end of the story.

I told Craig that all I knew about Mary's origins was that he was pulled from earth somewhere outside the Victorian town of Swan Hill. Craig led me outside to the hallway, where a tribal map of Australia was displayed. It was beautiful, a 200-piece patchwork of colours, but the only thing familiar was the map outline. I was staring into a country – or rather a collection of nations – I had never seen before. I looked for the state of Victoria and struggled to find where it started or ended. Each coloured patch blended organically into those around it; there were no neat pieces and no straight lines, the surveyor's straight edge was totally absent. Craig smiled as I struggled to navigate my way about a country that only a few minutes earlier I'd thought I knew so well – I was lost.

The patchwork pieces were much smaller and more numerous in the fertile floodplains of northern Victoria. Tribal names like Yorta Yorta, Wadi Wadi, and Nari Nari jumped out from beneath Craig's circling finger. He located Swan Hill, one of the few English placenames printed faintly on the map as a whitefella reference point.

'Mate,' Craig said slowly, his finger lightly tapping

the tiny spot on the southern banks of the Murray River, 'if he was dug up outside of Swan Hill, then there's a good chance he belongs to this mob.'

I had never read or heard of the name before. I said it aloud – 'Wamba Wamba' – and in their enunciation the two words would be forever forged into my own family's dreaming.

As we settled back into Craig's office a large figure sailed past the doorway.

'Rob! Got a sec?' Craig yelled into the wake left by the big man. 'That's Rob, he's the fella we need to speak to.'

A wild head of hair poked around the door. Craig recounted my story, and with each sentence Rob inched into the room like a bear being drawn out of the forest by the promise of honey. When Craig got to the part about the mantelpiece, Rob flinched as if he'd been stung on the nose.

'Wha-huh, how could anybody do such a thing?' he asked.

Craig shrugged and shook his head again. 'Listen, John, it's nothing personal, you're doing the right thing, but I just can't *imagine* keeping a skull on my mantelpiece. It's like me ringing up Rob here and saying, "Hey Rob, I've got the skull of a dead whitefella on my bookshelf, wanna come over and see?"'

The two men chuckled, and for the moment I felt a little better.

'Yeah,' said Rob, 'just imagine what the papers would say: "Savage headhunters display white man's head."'

I sat there, wondering how on earth I was going to bring up the subject with my father. I asked for some advice on how to approach him, some arguments that would help back up my case. Craig looked at me as if I had just asked the dumbest question of all time.

'What justification do you need? It's not yours. What your family has done is wrong.' Craig's tone was firm, but still, there was no animosity in his voice.

'Okay, okay.' His voice softened. 'You could talk about the dignity of the dead – you know, look at how much effort you whitefellas put into finding and bringing home lost servicemen from the various wars. It's the same thing.'

I nodded. As a paid-up RSL member, Dad *would* relate to that. Then Rob brought up the subject of curses. You only had to take one look at Rob to know he was a nice bloke with a big heart to match his sizeable frame, but he was clearly unsettled by the very thought that anyone would be foolish enough to keep human bones under their roof.

'Mate, have you been to Uluru and seen that pile of stones?'

I shook my head. With the wide eyes of someone who clearly believed in bad juju, Rob described the steady stream of packages that arrive at Uluru containing rocks returned by pilfering visitors.

'Those rocks come back from all corners of the world; there's a book full of the letters from people detailing the bad luck they have had and begging for forgiveness. The rangers don't know exactly what part of the park the rocks come from, so they add them to a pile out the back of the visitors' centre. It's a big bloody pile, brother!'

He shuddered visibly. 'If a little pebble from Uluru can bring bad luck, what kind of trouble do you think taking a skull from its country and keeping it in your home is gunna bring you?'

CHAPTER
FOUR

{ 20 SEPTEMBER 2005 }

I fished out a piece of paper from my wallet. On it were a couple of hastily scribbled numbers.

'Uncle Bob Weatherall, he's the expert in the business of repatriation up here,' Craig had told me before rattling off the numbers. I hoped they were correct; I'd been too nervous to ask Craig to repeat them.

The first number was for an organisation called FAIRA. A pleasant woman answered the phone and explained that the organisation had closed, but that someone came by every few weeks to collect the mail and messages. I phoned the next number and another woman, who I assumed was Uncle Bob's wife, told me that Bob was away on a fishing trip and wouldn't be back for at least a week. She gave me his mobile number, which I tried a couple of times only to receive the out-of-range message. I resigned myself to waiting until he returned.

After dinner I read my daughters their bedtime stories, but my mind was elsewhere. I settled in front of the computer and ran a search on 'Aboriginal', 'remains' and 'repatriation'. Pages and pages of results came up instantly. Before I knew it I was diving in and out of websites, trying to piece together some sort of understanding. Newspaper articles, academic papers, essays and links flashed before me. I was too impatient to read anything fully; if something looked relevant I hit the Print button or bookmarked it. The printer screamed for paper and fresh ink. I darted in and out of search results like a shark feeding on a cloud of silver mullet. The deeper I went, the greater the urgency I felt. A couple of hours later, I fell back in my chair, exhausted; I'd expected to find perhaps half a dozen obscure articles, but instead I'd waded into a cultural, political and emotional riptide.

There were articles about institutions stubbornly refusing to hand back collections of Aboriginal remains that sometimes numbered in the hundreds. And there were stories about personal collections, cobbled together by enthusiasts in garages and back-yard sheds. After a quick perusal of my random printouts, it dawned on me that the issue of repatriation didn't concern just a few hundred sets of remains, it was of a far greater magnitude – there were tens of thousands! The very scale of the issue was too mind-numbing to get my head around; images came into my head of those terrible expanses of bleached skulls on the Cambodian Killing Fields. Why? Why had so many Aboriginal remains been shipped off to the four corners of the globe? It seemed so utterly unreasonable that the British Museum needed – actually needed – 1570 sets of remains from Aboriginal men, women and children. Filed in specimen drawers, lined up in glass cases, stuffed into cabinets and crammed into never-to-be-opened boxes, locked in a dusty twilight zone far from country; these were human remains in limbo. And here *I* was, with just one skull tucked under my arm. What difference could one repatriation make?

As the torrent of information gushing from my

computer began to sweep away my resolve, there was one story that leapt out – one story about one tiny set of remains that helped me understand, and kept me anchored to my promise to Mary.

'The baby in the tree story' concerned the remains of an Aboriginal infant that had been discovered by a woodcutter in 1904 near the north-western Victorian town of Charlton. The tiny skeleton had been laid to rest in a tree hollow, lovingly wrapped in a possum-skin cloak with, as one newspaper described it, 'a dazzling array of rare treasures'. The Indigenous artefacts included over 100 wooden pegs used for staking out possum skins for drying, necklaces, a tool and weapons belt, and an emu-feather apron, as well as some European-made objects. So numerous were the artefacts, and such was the care with which the child and his possessions had been laid to rest, that it was believed the infant might have been the son or daughter of a tribal elder. The remains were handed to the National Museum of Victoria, where they were catalogued and assigned to drawers, and lay untouched for the next 90 years. As the twentieth century drew to a close there was a sudden renewal of interest in what became known as the Jaara Baby, by researchers and the Dja Dja Wurrung, the infant's traditional family group. Museum anthropologists were keen to discover whatever secrets the little prince might reveal, while his descendants wanted him put back to rest without delay. It was a tug of war between the sciences and the spiritual that continues to underpin the entire repatriation issue.

I put the articles and news clippings into chronological order and in the quiet midnight hours followed the Jaara Baby's journey from his burial place to the coroner's office and the museum, and back to a burial place known only to the Dja Dja Wurrung. The infant and his belongings were handed back to his people on 10 September 2003 – 99 years to the day after they were first discovered. As I read the story, I began to glean an understanding of just how deeply Aboriginal people respect their dead kin, and above all, of the importance of going home to country. I laid the wad of printouts on my bedside table and turned off the lamp; moonbeams swished overhead, chopped into even fragments by the blades of the ceiling fan. The timeless and the temporal – it somehow seemed like a weird metaphor for the story I had just read, for the last few days, for what was happening. But before I could think about it much more, I was asleep.

{ 21 SEPTEMBER 2005 }

'I've been thinking about that skull all week, I can't get it out of my head,' said the girl with the big eyes. A week had passed since I'd blurted out our family secret. At the mention of the skull, the eyes of all my classmates were again upon me. It was my moment. I explained that I'd spoken to some people about returning 'the remains' – a term it was suggested I use out of respect for the original tenant (the word 'skull' was just weighed down with too much horror-movie baggage). I detailed my encounters with Craig, Rob, the tree baby and the amazing patchwork map; it was as if I had just returned from a fleeting visit to a mystical, far-off land and was regaling my countrymen with tales of my wondrous adventures. After I had finished, my lecturer smiled and suggested to the class that they all take a leaf out of my book and go on a little positive adventure of their own before the next class in a fortnights time. A hot blush swept up my chest and over my face. My classmates didn't look particularly thrilled at the prospect of seeking out their own particular rabbit holes.

'Like what?' moaned a hirsute young fellow. 'John was lucky, his something was right under his nose.'

'Tell you what,' I said, glad for the chance to lighten

the mood, 'I haven't actually mentioned any of this to my father yet, perhaps *you'd* like to ask him to hand over the remains?'

There was a ripple of nervous laughter.

'Oh, we forgot about your dad,' said one of the girls. 'Perhaps you're not getting it so easy after all.'

'I'm not,' I said. 'Believe me, I'm not.'

{ 22 SEPTEMBER 2005 }

I'm not a little kid any more; I left home 20 years ago and now have two children of my own. Yet my father still has the unnerving ability – with a barely perceptible nostril twitch – to teleport me back into the shorts of a very nervous ten-year-old. I didn't spend my childhood in fear, far from it; in fact, my brother and I often got away with murder. But Dad wasn't one to tolerate fools, and if he was in one of his dark moods it was best to stay out of his way. And even when Dad was in a good mood, it often took only a trivial thing to set his highly combustible Greek temper alight. Little things on television – like a story on lefties, greenies or Aborigines – could set him off on a right-wing diatribe and it would have been reckless of us to do anything but nod in agreement.

These thoughts stampeded through my mind as I arrived at my parents' house to drop off my two-year-old daughter Lydia for the day. Even though my father had mellowed considerably over the last 30 years, it was the firebrand Dad of old who occupied my thoughts as I fumbled Lydia's lunchbox and bottles into the fridge. I waited for my moment in the kitchen, struggling to look casual while Mum fussed over my daughter. Eventually Lydia scampered off down the hallway and Mum gave chase; Dad and I were alone at last.

'Dad, I wanted to discuss something with you.' There was no turning back now. 'It's sort of a delicate matter.'

My father was caught off guard. I'd rarely addressed him so seriously before, and I'm sure he thought I was about to hit him up for a loan – or worse. He tensed in mid-step and turned to me. He took a breath, as if to remind himself that his son – someone he'd spent 20 years telling what to do – was now a man. I took a deeper breath and reminded myself of the same thing. The father–son patterns of a lifetime creaked aside in painful slowness and let this new moment through. And then for the first time I realised – marvelled – at how much older he had become; I was now taller and he shorter. Still, I didn't feel any braver.

'It's about the skull, you know, Mary. Well, I've been thinking . . .'

I became acutely aware of every change in my father's face; every pore in his skin seemed magnified. One eyebrow rose a quarter of a millimetre, his nostril hairs fluttered, but it wasn't enough to throw me off course. I told Dad about my study of indigenous writing, the feelings I'd been having about Mary, and what I'd learnt about repatriation. His cropped grey hair bristled, but he was no longer the fearsome drill sergeant I remembered as a child. For years Dad had insisted that my brother and I wear crewcuts just like his. 'If it's good enough for the US Marines, it's good enough for you two,' he'd bark at my brother and me. One day he bought a home barbering kit. Dad may have been a fine veterinarian, but somehow he got the idea that shaving dogs' bellies prior to operations qualified him as a gentleman's hairdresser. It didn't. How cold my head felt after each 'number one'. When I see those old World War II photos of the French women who collaborated with the Germans being publicly shaved in the streets, I feel a certain connection. My brother and I hid out under matching terry-towelling hats for weeks after every haircut, and were even granted permission to wear them in class! The clippers mysteriously disappeared one day, which I suspected Mum may have had a hand in.

He was still listening. Dad's exterior may have been as tough as an old stockman's boot, but inside beat the heart of a passionate and sensitive man.

'You know, Dad,' I said, beginning to probe for cracks in the boot leather, 'I wouldn't want your noggin sitting on someone's mantelpiece in England.'

'That's different, we're family,' he snapped. 'Mary's lot are long gone.'

I explained the little I understood about the Aboriginal concept of family and how it's much broader than ours. He was getting annoyed; and I could almost hear him thinking, 'What sort of bullshit are they teaching at university these days?'

It was then I pulled out my clincher, the one Craig had suggested. 'Look, Dad, it's no different to *us* bringing home our lost soldiers, sailors and pilots from where they fell in far-off lands. Just think of how much money and effort goes into those repatriations, sometimes just for a few teeth and a set of dogtags.'

His shoulders slumped, not in defeat, but because

he couldn't be bothered arguing over old bones. 'Ohhh, you can have it, it means nothing to me.'

'Well, it *will* mean a lot to its people,' I said, trying to hide my grin. 'Thanks, Dad, thanks.'

I noticed Mum on the sidelines; she'd been listening in and looked worried.

'We're not going to get into any trouble, are we?'

'Mum, they'll just be happy to get him back,' I reassured her, promising – or rather hoping – that there would be no legal implications.

I asked Dad where Mary had come from, but he couldn't tell me any more than I already knew – which wasn't a lot. He promised to ask his brother for more details. I decided not to push any more, we'd covered enough ground for one day!

Mum started looking around the mantelpiece. 'I can't remember where we put it.'

She seemed a little flustered; I sensed she was looking forward to getting Mary out of the house after all these years. I played doggo; it didn't feel like the right moment to announce that I'd already rifled through half the contents of the house.

'We'll dig it out later,' said Dad, returning to his morning paper. 'I'll let you know when we find it.'

Once home, I sat at my desk and surveyed the folders neatly laid out before me – university subjects, illustration projects, they all demanded my attention; but instead I was drawn to the telephone. I couldn't wait for Uncle Bob to return from his fishing trip. I felt as though a hand was inside me, pushing me forward. My first call was to the Queensland Museum. I was put though to a lifeless young woman from the Indigenous Collection. Speaking with her was like trying to suck sap from a 100-year-old telephone pole. Her boss was away on a field trip.

'Ring the Mines Department,' she suggested in an uninterested monotone.

'Mines Department?' I felt insulted; what did she think Mary was, a lump of coal?

'Yes, the mining operations are always ripping up burial sites. Ring them,' she said blankly and then hung up.

I looked up the number and introduced myself to the chirpy young girl on the switchboard.

'Oh my god! Are you serious, you want to return a skull?' Her voice darkened with suspicion. 'Sa-a-ay, you're not calling from a radio station are you? Do I win a prize or something for not getting tricked?'

I assured her that she wasn't going out live to air and that I wasn't a hoax caller. She seemed disappointed.

'A skull, yeah, like, a human one?' She sounded unconvinced but agreed to put me through to her supervisor. Two supervisors and three departments later I was connected to someone in an environmental unit. After listening to my story, the environmental officer called out to his colleague, 'Hey, Bill, I've got a bloke here who wants to return an Aboriginal skull.'

'A skull,' asked the colleague, 'where's the rest of it?'

'You there?' the officer asked me. 'Where's the rest of it?'

'As far as I know, still buried,' I answered, feeling as though I'd stumbled into a Monty Python skit.

'Still pushin' up daisies,' the officer called to his colleague.

'Why's he asking us then?' asked Bill.

'The Museum told him we had a department that looks after bones 'n' stuff.'

I heard a groan in the background.

'Tell him to ring Trevor, he might know.'

'Might be best to talk to Trevor,' Bill explained,

sounding relieved to have passed the hot potato into yet another part of the building. 'Hang about while I dig out his number.'

Five minutes later, my shoulders slumped as Trevor's answering machine clicked in.

'Hello, this is the message service for Trevor—. I'm on fieldwork for two weeks and won't be returning to my desk until—' I put the phone down. The Mines Department; it just didn't feel right. It sounded cold and undignified, as if the bones were being reduced to their mineral makeup, devoid of spirit. Anyway, Trevor sounded like a boof-head.

I spent the following three hours dialling numbers. I felt like a crazed rat in a laboratory maze, able to smell the cheese but too addle-headed to find it. I felt driven by something not of me; I ran on clumsy intuition, ignoring the leads that didn't feel right, side-stepping, hopping from one lead to another. There was little empathy from the people I spoke to; one minute I was made to feel as though I was trying to return a lost umbrella, the next like a blood-sucking ghoul.

Finally, *finally*, some kind soul at the National Museum suggested that I call the Melbourne Museum. Looking back it seems painfully obvious and logical that my first call should have been to the Melbourne Museum, but it wasn't. Perhaps I was forced to run though the labyrinth for a reason. An internet search led me to the museum's Indigenous collection and a name. I dialled the number, hoping that this person wouldn't be away on fieldwork, on long-service leave, or a moron. Simon answered on the second ring. He listened quietly as I told my story. Even though he'd only said three or four words, there was a reassuring calmness coming from his end of the line that encouraged me to take my time.

He let me catch my breath after I'd finished.

'Well you've phoned the right place, *if* they are Victorian remains. I don't suppose you have any idea where the cranium came from?'

'They came from just outside of Swan Hill,' I explained. 'I've been studying the maps and I'm pretty sure it's from Wamba Wamba country.'

There was an audible intake of breath on the other end of the phone; a sort of sucking noise – not fear or shock, something more like astonishment. I heard him mutter to himself, a barely audible few words slipping through the earpiece like wisps of smoke: 'weird . . . can't believe . . . just keeps happening'.

Simon returned from his private thoughts.

'John,' he said evenly, 'are you sitting down?'

'Mmmm, yes,' I lied, more intrigued by Simon's curious reaction than concerned with finding a comfy chair.

Simon explained that the day before he'd received a fax from the Wamba Wamba tribal council informing the Museum that a reburial had been scheduled to take place on Wamba Wamba land in two weeks time.

'How often do these reburials take place?' I asked, imagining that they were a regular occurrence.

'Almost never,' Simon answered, 'at least not like this one. Every so often a single set of remains might go back into the ground, you know, quietly, but this one's big. Thirty sets have been returned from different institutions from all over Australia and as far away as Scotland.'

We talked some more and Simon promised to get back to me the next day with the telephone number of one of the elders.

'They'll be *very* interested in your story.'

After the call, I sat in the kitchen and stared through the louvred windows that opened to the back yard. Rainbow lorikeets twittered amid the bright yellow explosions of golden penda flowers, bees droned about the nectar-laden coils of grevillea. In that moment of contemplation, in that neutral space between the whirling gears of thought, I understood the perfect synchronicity of it all; the pushing feeling, the fax, the reburial in two weeks. Mary's people were going home and he wanted to go too! I phoned Dad and excitedly filled him in on developments. As usual, my mind raced ahead of my mouth and I announced that I might fly Mary to Melbourne and hand him over personally. There was a gruff silence, then, 'Christ, son, you're going to a hell of a lot of trouble for an old Abo skull.'

CHAPTER FIVE

{ 23 SEPTEMBER 2005 }

The next morning, Simon from the Melbourne Museum phoned as promised. He'd been in touch with the Wamba Wamba elders. 'They're thrilled that another of their people is going home, they're over the moon.'

Simon gave me a name and phone number.

'Thank you, John,' he said, 'and *please* pass on my thanks to your mother and father.' It wasn't a hollow, greeting-card thank-you, it was one of those rare thank-yous that remind you what a powerful combination those two words can be.

I nervously phoned the number, expecting to hear something like the gravelly, earth-weathered voice of Skippy's Tara. Instead a young man answered with a breathless energy that suggested his life was a full one. Caught off guard, I opened my mouth and the voice of a stranger oozed forth; my tone lacked any sense of warmth, completely at odds with the way I truly felt. I sounded like a hard-nosed property developer negotiating a transfer of land rather than human remains. I sensed a negative energy in the phone line. Then Jason explained that it was a bad time to talk, there'd been a death in the community that he had to attend to, but he promised to get back to me soon.

What a letdown; I'd been expecting my first contact with Mary's people to be something special – magical, even. Later on I phoned Dad to pass on Simon's thanks. He grunted in that stubborn Greek way of his and moved the conversation on to something else.

{ 24–25 SEPTEMBER 2005 }

I waited all weekend for Jason to call. Nothing. Mum phoned on Sunday evening while Dad was out and told me how happy she was that Mary was going home.

'Your grandmother would be just so, so pleased.'

The words caught in her throat. 'Do you remember when she used to visit, the first thing she'd do was take a clean teatowel from the kitchen drawer and place it carefully over Mary. Remember how annoyed she used to get with your father and uncle – "The poor devil should be back with his own people," she used to say.' My mother doesn't often get emotional but when she does it comes from a very deep place and means all the more. Her words steadied my uncertain spirit and gave me the reassurance I needed.

{ 26 SEPTEMBER 2005 }

I dropped the kids at my parents' place. In the background the morning show ping-ponged between serious news and inane chatter.

'I've spoken to your uncle,' said Dad, handing me a sheet of notepaper with the details of where Mary had been unearthed. The location was precise: the Old Kannon Property, 15 kilometres east of Swan Hill on the New South Wales side of the Murray River.

'There he is.' He nodded to a plastic shopping bag on the dining-room table. 'Found him in the old TV cupboard.'

That evening I returned home from uni with two

tired kids and Mary. My wife Stella greeted me with the news that a Wamba Wamba elder, Jason's uncle, had phoned earlier in the day; his name was Gary Murray.

'What'd he say, what's he sound like?' I pumped Stella for every little detail while the girls ran around us squawking for their dinner.

'He sounded really nice,' said Stella.

'What else, anything else?'

'There is nothing else, he's just really happy about getting Mary back and looks forward to talking to you. The number's up by the phone.'

'And he sounded nice, yeah?'

'Really nice.'

The number by the phone was a mobile number. A mobile phone; although I instantly realised how ridiculous the thought was, my concept of an Aboriginal elder didn't include modern technology. My idea of an elder was of an old guy sitting cross-legged in red dust with didgeridoo music droning in the background, in a place untouched by personalised ringtones and SMS. Gary answered the phone, and he didn't sound like Tara either, or old. My damned conditioning!

Gary's voice was deep and his sentences were short and uncluttered; he spoke the way people from the bush tend to talk. He was instantly likeable.

'How's this for timing,' he said. 'Unreal, isn't it!'

Gratitude poured from the earpiece; there was not a hint of reproach or judgement in his voice. Gary asked if I was absolutely positive that Mary was from Wamba Wamba country. I explained that my uncle found it on the Old Kannon farm, which according to the maps was well within his clan's territory.

'I'll have to check,' he replied 'but I think that's the old name of the property right next door to Menera.'

'Menera?' I asked.

'Yeah, that's the name of the property we bought, Menera Station, seven kilometres of prime river front-age, it belongs to the Wamba Wamba again.' Gary's words unrolled like a soft fabric woven with his love of country. 'It's just the start; we've got big plans for the place. That's where the reburial's taking place, right in the most beautiful part of the property. Farmers keep the best land for crops, we keep the best bits for burying our people. It's beautiful, you come down and I'll show it to you – beautiful.'

I was having trouble taking it all in; I'd always imagined that Mary would be returned by post, or that maybe I'd fly to Melbourne and hand it over personally at the Museum. I hadn't given any thought to what might happen after that. Now I was not only getting a description of Mary's country, I was being transported there through Gary's voice.

'Let me get this right,' I said. 'Where the remains are going to be reburied, it's quite possible he once walked over the same ground – I mean, this is his back yard?'

Gary laughed. 'That's it, he's coming home, that's for sure.'

I felt an incredible stillness, as if all the air had been sucked out of the room.

'You tell your old man how much the Wamba Wamba Nation appreciates what he's doing; in the meantime I've got some other business to attend to, we've had another death in the clan, but I'll be back in touch soon.'

After dinner I googled Gary Murray. His name had sounded familiar, and sure enough there he was, right at the forefront of the Jaara Baby repatriation! His name popped up everywhere – if there was a story about cultural theft or the repatriation of Victorian Indigenous remains, there was a good chance that

Gary's name would be mentioned. I ran an image search and followed a link until he filled my screen. In the picture, Gary was wrapped up to his neck in some sort of patchwork fur cloak. He wore an Akubra hat pulled down low, his face a mixture of determination and defiance. His eyes stared right into the barrel of the camera lens. He held a large piece of bark – like a shield – embellished with the worn carving of a dancer, legs and arms spread wide to a world of animals and fish. It looked as old as the oldest cave paintings in Europe.

If I hadn't had such a friendly chat a few moments ago with this man I would have been very nervous about meeting him. He looked like a warrior. I clicked on the photo to save it to my desktop; the file reduced neatly into a little icon onto my cluttered screen, and it was then that I got my first hateful taste of racism, what it means, what it does. Underneath the folder symbol appeared the photo caption: ABO. Rather than using Gary's name, the journalist or photo editor had typed in a generic derogatory slur that he thought no one would ever see. Straight away I understood the defiance in Gary's photograph, and I began to appreciate the anger behind the countless raised fists I'd seen in Aboriginal demonstrations and protests on the nightly news.

It was such a small – some would say insignificant – act, yet for me it demonstrated how the insidious hate worm of racism works. And this example was in one of the nation's leading newspapers! Racism reduces the individual to a caricature; it undermines the power of story by pushing preconditioned buttons – primarily fear. In this photo Gary stood strong in culture and as a man, yet here was this slur attempting to kick his legs out from beneath him. People often say 'It's only a word,' but language is a powerful force. As an Australian of Greek descent who weathered the taunts of 'wog boy' throughout my childhood, I remember the feeling of relief when the bedraggled Vietnamese boat people started washing up onto our shores in the late 1970s. Suddenly the attention shifted from wogs to the newly arrived slopes and geeks. Yet despite the ever-shifting focus of racism in this country, Indigenous Australians have continuously occupied the bottom rung of the ladder. And all too often, when their hands reached up to the next rung, it was the hobnailed boot of language that stomped on fingers of self-determination.

{ 27 SEPTEMBER 2005 }

The alarm clock bleeped. I jumped out of bed and almost out of my skin with excitement; I needed to talk about the reburial. I watched the clock through breakfast. I knew Craig would be at work at 9 a.m., but I took a chance and phoned half an hour earlier. He answered immediately. I spluttered the news of the reburial into the mouthpiece.

'Mate, Mary is going back into the same ground, the *same* ground he used to walk on, the same side of the river even!'

Craig was pleased, but remained calm. 'Mate, there are big wheels turning in the universe that we haven't even begun to understand yet.'

I could only agree. After the call I closed my eyes and for a moment I could *feel* those big wheels turning like constellations, unstoppable in their tidal force. Since deciding to return Mary, doors had been flying open before me. Something was going on, 'it' was all around me, but if I looked too hard it vanished.

I made my way to the desk and tried to concentrate on my work and studies, but it was impossible to stay focused. I looked up my uncle's number; like my father, he was a veterinarian and the two had shared a practice together for over 20 years, but since their retirement I'd rarely seen him. He seemed happy to hear from me and had heard of my efforts to have Mary returned. As a man of science and medicine, he was a little bemused by all the fuss being made over some old bones. My uncle was a country vet fresh out of veterinary school when he started his practice in Swan Hill in 1966, and like my father he spent much of his time calling on farms.

'There were bones everywhere along the Murray,' he explained. 'Before we came along, the Riverine plains supported the highest concentration of blacks in the country.'

My uncle described the vast networks of irrigation channels that were gouged through the earth to draw water from the Murray River into the distant fields. Excavation machines called 'rippers' would tear open the earth in long lines, often opening up burial sites.

'These burial sites were often in raised mounds called camp ovens,' he explained. 'When the Murray flooded, which it did every year, the blacks would camp on these ovens; I saw some that were bloody huge. Well, if a blackfella died during a flood they had to put the body somewhere, so they planted it in the camp oven.'

I asked why they were called camp ovens.

'Well, I guess they were really midden heaps, like the ones you find along the coasts – they're a build-up of thousands of years of shell and bone, leftovers really. The mounds are just shell-grit and ash. They'd dig a firepit in it and do all their cooking there. Sometimes they'd cover the food over and do a slow cook using big clay balls to hold the heat.'

'Like a Maori *hangi*?' I asked.

'That's it. You can still find the clay balls all over the place. But the thing about these camp ovens is that they drained really quickly – because they were mainly ash and shell-grit – so bones and artefacts tended to be really well preserved. Things buried in normal soil break down much quicker.'

My uncle explained that one night in a Swan Hill pub he'd mentioned a recently ripped open mound to a young pathologist.

'This young fella begged me to take him out to the farm, so a few days later I took him out. There were bones all over the place. He thought it was Christmas,' my uncle chuckled. 'That's when I decided to souvenir a couple too, and that's how Mary ended up on your old man's wall unit.'

'So, you didn't have to notify anybody?' I asked.

'No!' My uncle scoffed at the question. 'Burial sites were being ripped open and ploughed up all over the place. Sometimes a farmer might feel a little guilty about it and leave a few sugarbags of bones by the police station at night.'

'So what did the police do?' I was hanging on my uncle's every word by now.

'Loaded 'em up into the paddy wagon and took 'em to the rubbish tip,' he replied.

'The dump! You mean they just chucked them in with everyone's garbage?' I imagined bags of skulls lying amid stinking kitchen scraps and broken toys. 'My god, people were allowed to scrounge in those days, imagine coming across . . .' My voice trailed off as I imagined someone – a child – peeking into an inviting-looking sugarbag.

My uncle chuckled again. 'No, it wasn't like that, they had a quiet corner set aside for blackfellas' bones.'

I breathed the slightest sigh of relief and wondered what had become of that 'quiet corner' now; had the dump been developed? Was there now a house on top of all those remains, a sporting field, a school?

My uncle was on a roll now; we talked about his experiences with the Aboriginal people who lived in the camps outside Swan Hill.

'They used to come into town for grog mostly. At first I used to get angry with the shopkeepers and publicans. I'd say, 'Why are you selling them this booze, can't you see it's killing the poor bastards?' But I was young, new in town; you learn to accept things the way they are.' A sadness began to weigh down on what until then had been happy reminiscences. 'I saw too many things, too many – I guess it just makes you switch off.' My uncle was a larger-than-life character; in his prime he'd travelled the world and mixed it with the big boys – he'd been a player. But I'd never heard him speak like that before; I'd never heard his voice falter.

{ 28 SEPTEMBER 2005 }

The ceiling fan churned hot air. My daughters were in bed. Crickets buzzed; but it was only when they paused to pant in the sticky night that I noticed them. The lights of Brisbane's CBD hummed silently, but you could feel a transfer of energy drawn from the midnight earth into filaments and glass that rose up in the distance. The carpet-snake river curved though it all in timeless twists, cooling its tongue in the sea. Good god! It was starting to get to me, this other way of seeing.

Gary was on the other end of the phone, half a continent away in Melbourne. Our conversation came easily, naturally. I'd been holding back a couple of details about the skull – about Mary – but Gary sounded cool, relaxed.

My first concern was the name, Mary; I'd been worrying that by calling a male – albeit a deceased one – by a female name, my family had been disrespectful, or even worse was breaking some sort of taboo. Gary laughed when I made my first confession. 'Mate, at least you gave him a name, you humanised him, you respected him. Most of the remains we get back are tagged with a serial number, like army dogtags – only there's no name, just a number, like the numbers the Germans tattooed on the arms of the Jewish people in the Holocaust. It's a beautiful thing that you and your family cared enough about my ancestor to give him a name.'

'Well, there's another thing,' I continued, feeling a little more at ease, 'Mary is kind of, well . . . yellow.'

I almost whispered the last word. I explained that Dad had given Mary a liberal coat of lacquer every couple of years to preserve the bone, and now, 40 years later, it had taken on a yellow – almost golden – patina. Gary laughed again.

'And there's a tiny piece of wood glued to the back of the skull to stop it rolling backwards, but it's only the size of a matchbox and Dad's stained it to make it look nice. I thought about tapping it off gently with a hammer before returning it, but I'm worried bits of bone might break off with it.'

'Listen, mate, don't worry about it, just leave it as it is, I'm just so glad your old man made the effort to keep the old fella in one piece. Yellow.' He chuckled again. 'John, I've gone into houses where the skull's been wrapped up in metal and wire to keep it together. I've had skulls returned with all sorts of right-wing neo-Nazi shit written all over them. People have used the top parts for ashtrays and mulling bowls – I even saw one wearing a rasta hat with a big fat joint sticking out of its mouth.'

My mind flicked back to Mary with a Winfield Blue balancing where a tooth should have been. 'Oh, people did that?' I said sheepishly.

'Listen, mate, we don't care what the story is, we're just happy to get our old people back. Listen, I'm coming up to collect the old fella. Tell your old man I'd like to buy him a beer, I really want to thank him for taking such good care of Mary. We really owe you for this one, we owe you big time.'

After the call, I sat on the front steps looking out through the trees at the city lights. The gum trees danced in a swaying motion, leafy boughs raised to the heavens like shamans' arms. How strange, I thought; I should be apologising to these people for everything I've taken from them, and here they are thanking me, saying *they owe me.*

CHAPTER
SIX

The bicycle is my totem. I first learnt to ride on a cattle property in central Queensland. As a vet, Dad did contract work all over the state, mostly blood-testing on cattle. Mum, my little brother and I would wake in the pre-dawn and take Dad out to the airfield in Brisbane where we'd say our goodbyes and watch him climb into a tiny twin-engined aeroplane. Dad always attempted to look a little sad as he hugged Mum and gave her backside a squeeze, but you could tell he was excited to be going bush again. My parents grew up in the country, and they are still country people at heart despite having lived in the city for over 40 years. Smelling of Old Spice aftershave, Dad would kiss my brother and me. And when we saw him again, days, sometime weeks later, his face would be bristly grey and smell of campfires and the clean red earth.

Dad always returned with treasures. Sometimes he'd bring back lumps of petrified wood – chunks of wood so old it had turned to stone. My brother and I would turn these million-year-old bits of tree over in our hands and marvel at the thought that a dinosaur might have rubbed its itchy behind against this very bit of tree trunk. Other times he'd delve into an old beer carton and produce Aboriginal implements like stone axe-heads, black and beautifully smooth. My brother and I would hold them, smell them. Cold and incredibly hard, they had a sense of the eternal about them. We instinctively knew where and how to hold these objects and it boggled our minds to think that we were the first people to touch them in a hundred, perhaps a thousand, years. Once Dad found a stone axe – its handle still attached – embedded into the trunk of a tree, as if its owner had just had enough, driven it into the wood and walked away. My father was as tough as nails, yet my brother and I were in awe of this man who seemed to us to be a cross between Indiana Jones and Dr Dolittle.

When I turned seven or eight it was announced that I was old enough to join my father on one of his shorter trips. I climbed aboard the tiny Beechcraft Baron. The pilot wore a starched white shirt with frayed epaulettes and a jaunty captain's cap. We flew away from the green coast, across the Dividing Range and over the wide brown plains of western Queensland. From 5000 feet, the squiggly waterways and blotchy dots of vegetation looked like the Aboriginal paintings my grandmother had shown me in books. It still strikes me as incredible that these earthbound people could paint the landscape from the view of an eagle riding the highest thermals.

For three days I helped my father test cattle. Three or four hundred head were herded each day through the stockyards. As each beast lumbered down a narrow crush, a pair of iron gates swung down and clamped its neck, holding it securely. Dad would swiftly lift the tail of the animal, make a little nick with his scalpel and fill a small plastic sample bottle with blood. My job was to pass fresh bottles to Dad, screw the cap back on and record the animal's number onto the lid. The days were hot and filled with the stench of splattering cow manure, but there were bonuses, like being allowed to use the electric cattle prod and bouncing around the property in the back of a ute as it made its way to and from the stockyards each day. But the best bonus of all was the farmer's daughter's bicycle. It was an old Speedwell clunker; a girl's bike without a crossbar. I had eyed it off at the homestead as I kicked around the dusty yard while the adults enjoyed afternoon tea under the shade of a tree. The farmer had noticed me sizing up the bicycle and called out, 'It's a bit big, but go on, have a go.'

I was a demon on a trike, but I'd never ridden a two-wheeler and this was several sizes too large. I managed to get the old rattler moving by just riding up and down on the pedals in a standing position; the bike was so big that the nose of the saddle kept bumping into the small of my back. If it had been a boy's bike with a crossbar (or nut-crusher as we used to call them) the bike would have stayed where it was. I wobbled around the house and past the adults.

'Well, I'll be buggered, the little fella's riding it!' came a voice from behind the steaming billy tea and pumpkin scones. My chest swelled with pride. Round and round I went, each time with greater confidence and speed. Soon I was riding the long 300-metre driveway up to the front gate and back. Up and back, up and back. I was in heaven and I was determined not to stop, not to get off, until I'd made a suitable impression on my father.

We never asked Dad for anything; the trick with him was to plant a seed, and once it sprouted, to let him think that it was all his idea. Up and down the driveway I went. After half an hour my hands were raw from the hard plastic grips, my back screamed, and my brand-new gym boots blistered my feet. I didn't get off until the farmer had remarked to my father at least three times, 'Crikey, look at the little fella go, could have ridden into town and back by now.'

Galahs wheeled in the big sky and a rusty windmill creaked in the slow-motion breeze as the tyres imprinted their wobbly story upon the earth. That night in bed, like a sailor back on land after a long voyage, I was still rolling, still rattling, still turning over those big cranks. I've been riding ever since.

{ 2 OCTOBER 2005 }

Thirty-three years later I was on the saddle of my latest bike; down in the cool gullies behind Mt Coot-tha. I was with friends; it was early – somewhere between 6 and 7 a.m. My legs have pedalled so many bikes. Shortly after we returned from that trip to the bush, my father brought me home my first bike – a speckly red Tom Wallace Special. Years later came the dragster, then the BMX bike. The first bike I paid for was a baby-poo-brown 12-speed racing bike. Then came the mountain bikes – six or seven of them bought, sold and traded in search of the perfect ride. Now here I was, a man of 39, flying like a ten-year-old down the well-packed ribbon of dirt that formed the trail. I usually ride last in a bunch; I am not the fastest and I tend to slow the more aggressive riders down. I like it at the back, where I don't have to worry about the nipping tyres of others. But on this morning I was out in front with Matt and Steve following.

We dropped into a section of single track at 20-second intervals – like parachutists. The track followed a creek, alternating between coils of giddy hairpins and ha-ha-humps of rollercoaster joy. Suddenly the track disappeared as a huge black-and-red mass of feathers swooped down in front of me, almost clipping the top of my helmet. It squawked in an otherworldly 'Kar-aak', shocking me out of my waking slumber. The bird slipped down the track three or four bike lengths ahead of me at chest height. With the slightest wingtip correction this way and that it followed the track with slot-car precision. And the sound its wings made – they rippled the way taut flags ripple in a strong wind, only this sound was alive – fat! We flew together in unison; at times I might as well have been hang-gliding beneath him.

The track took a sharp dogleg and then zigzagged though a narrow stand of trees; it was tight, just wide enough for a crouching rider. The bird zipped though the gaps with cocky ease and then, clearing the thicket, floated up, up, up and with the last of his momentum touched down on the branch of a young gum tree. His perch lurched earthward under his great weight before rebounding, nearly sending him heavenward again.

'Karak, karak!' he called as his wobbly perch settled.

He watched me watching him, then groomed himself a little, his finger-like grey tongue gaggling in and out of a black beak that looked as powerful as a mud-crab's claw. My two friends burst through the thicket and rolled to a stop. Their eyes followed mine. As if on cue, the black cockatoo stretched out his plumage, revealing his bright red markings.

'Kar-aak,' he screeched to his growing audience.

'A Red-tailed Black Cockatoo!' said Steve. 'They're everywhere up north, but this is the first I've seen in Brisbane.'

'I've *never* seen one before, what a beauty,' said Matt.

'Me neither. He was flying down the track right in front of me, just like that.' I mimicked the bird's flight with splayed-out fingers.

We stood about, straddling our bikes, enjoying the coolness of the hollow and the company of our new friend. Eventually, Steve clipped back into his pedals and continued down the track. Matt followed a minute later, leaving me with the cockatoo. He groomed his glossy coat while I made silly clicking birdcall noises. We had shared a special moment, but in true human fashion, I wanted more. Instead of just allowing the moment to be, I had broken the spell. With a great flap he flew to the higher branch of an adjacent tree. The foliage wobbled and rustled under his weight. I clicked my tongue again and he was gone.

Later that day I was on my bike again. The Brisbane River rolled by like a long bolt of sequined fabric. On the opposite bank the central business district rose in concrete and glass self-importance, its pretensions made ludicrous by a happy sun. Everything felt clear and clean, the river ducted breezes inland from the bay, carrying the scent of whitecaps, crabpots and plywood pleasure craft. The organisers of the Brisbane Writers Festival who had pitched marquees and café umbrellas on the riverbank outside the State Library had had their perfect-weather wishes granted. I chained my bike to a lamp-post and surveyed the festival program. One of the requirements for my Indigenous Writing unit was to go to a couple of sessions at the Writers Festival featuring Indigenous writers.

I made my way to a marquee where two Wik storytellers were scheduled to speak. Once inside I was surprised to see a large banner pronouncing that the session was sponsored by a mining company. The tent was three-quarters full and few of the faces were white. I'd heard the name Wik – like Mabo – numerous times in the media, I knew it had something to do with an important native title claim a few years ago and I remembered that the Wik people were from somewhere on Cape York Peninsula, but that's all I knew. And then it dawned on me that until recently, Wik was one of the only tribal names I knew! I knew that Aborigines from Queensland broadly referred to themselves as Murries, and that in southern states they used the term Kooris, and sure, when I'd looked at the Aboriginal map some of the names rang a dim little bell in the back of my brain. But there I was, sitting near a bend in the Brisbane River that had been in continual use as a traditional meeting place for thousands of years, and I didn't even know the name of the tribe whose cooking-fire smoke and laughter had once filled the space in which I now sat. Zulu, Bantu, Masai, Swahili, Hottentot, Apache, Cherokee, Pawnee, Arapahoe, Navaho – I knew the names of more African and American tribal nations than Australian!

A young guy from my class entered hesitantly, awkwardly – as I did. He looked relieved to see my familiar face and plonked beside me. Moments later three girls from the class breezed in. We all clumped together. The girls chirped enthusiastically about other sessions they had been to. A festival volunteer flitted about, checking that the PA was working and that everything was just so before ushering in the two speakers. Before the session began, the two storytellers, Fiona Doyle and her kin sister Alyson set out on the table before them an array of Wik tools and handicrafts. The centrepiece was an extraordinary headdress, an explosion of black and orange feathers.

'Wow!' I whispered to my neighbour. 'That headdress is just astonishing.'

I was mesmerised by the feathers, spellbound. Were they from the same species of bird I'd seen that morning, the black cockatoo? Fanned out in majestic order, they seemed to possess an otherworldly energy. I shivered in my hard plastic seat.

Fiona spoke about her childhood in Wik country and then introduced Auntie Alyson. The woman might have been 50 or 80, it was impossible to tell. Her hair was a pure grey Afro that seemed to vibrate as if it had an electric current running through it. She took her time speaking, taking long breaks between sentences; she slowed down our big-city heart-rates and pulled us into her story. I'm not sure I really heard anything properly; rather, it was a feeling that she imparted, a sense of place. Her words were measured, like footsteps that took us on a long walk, and when she laughed at her own jokes it was like little lightning cracks flashing on the horizon. Piece by piece she held up and explained her collection; the dillybags, baskets and bowls, and the headdress. She brought each of them to life; these were not dusty museum relics but pieces of living culture, works of art and tools of survival all rolled into one. They were contemporary pieces that Wik men, women and children had made and used, just as their ancestors used to do – not the product of some far-off factory. I looked out through the tent flaps and watched people of my white world wandering by, and wondered how many of us could, with our own hands, craft the tools that would enable us to live off the land. I looked at these durable implements that came quietly from Nature and would return quietly to Nature. Then I thought of our modern tools for living, so complex yet often so lacking craftsmanship; and so disposable, sometimes consigned to festering landfill after a single season, sometimes after a single use.

One other thing about Auntie Alyson's talk that stuck in my mind, probably because it surprised me so, was that she kept singing the praises of the big mining company that operated in Wik country. She spoke of the training programs that gave the young men hope and got them out of the dependency cycle. She spoke of the money invested in cultural programs. She thanked the company for flying her down from Wik country to speak to us. I'd always thought that in terms of respecting the land and the traditional owners, big mining companies were the bad guys. In this case at least, I was very ill-informed. Another preconception popped.

After the talk, I made my way up to the front of the marquee to have a closer look at the feather headdress; could these feathers be from the same kind of bird I'd flown with that morning – the black cockatoo? The orange splotches on the jet-black plumage weren't nearly as red as those I'd seen on Mount Coot-tha. Perhaps they'd faded? Aunty Alyson and Fiona were off to one side, talking to a gaggle of enthusiastic women who'd hurried up at the end of the session. I edged closer, keen to talk, eager to ask questions about the headdress. I began to overhear the discussion taking place; knowledgeable questions were being asked by people who seemed to know infinitely more than I.

The way the conversation flowed only magnified my unease. As laughter radiated from the group I was again pulled down by the weight of my own baggage. I reached out, gently touched the headdress, and left.

CHAPTER
SEVEN

I spent a lot of time in the bush when I was growing up
– hunting, fishing, visiting properties and camping –
but never once did I see any Aborigines. Sometimes
I imagined that they were there, in the bush, watching
us, only to slip back behind the grasstrees as I turned to
look. I know I felt a presence, as if they had sensed our
arrival and moved on only moments before. Sometimes
I would see their spirit faces in the gnarled bunions that
grew on the sides of trees, or on rocky escarpments that

in a certain slant of light looked like the frozen faces of Dreamtime heroes. The Aborigines of my childhood existed only in an imagination drawing on books, films and kitsch. The real ones had been corralled onto the missions and communities of Cherbourg, Woorabinda and Palm Island, or lived in the poorer suburbs that fringed the cities and towns.

{ 3 OCTOBER 2005 }

I spied Big Rob at the uni refectory. He saw me and waved me over. Rob was having lunch with a young Aboriginal girl who took one look at me and quickly excused herself – in fact she almost ran off. Most likely she was an upset student having a meltdown. But my overactive imagination told me that she'd heard about 'the ghoul with the skull' and suddenly there I was in the flesh, swooping in. Whatever the reason for her hasty departure, I'd begun to realise that Aboriginal people *feel* death very differently to white folk. It's as though death is almost a *living* thing; a very real ongoing energy.

Rob listened intently as I filled him in on all the latest developments; his big frame visibly shivered a number of times. And then he did the weirdest thing. He asked me to say my surname slowly, and then he repeated it a number of times: Dan-al-is, Dan-al-is. He explained that he was committing my name to memory. 'Big things are going to come from this business. I think maybe you'll write a book about all this.'

Rob had no idea that I'd written a couple of children's picture books. I'd long entertained the idea of writing something more grown-up, but the idea of writing about Mary seemed almost perverse.

'Your life is going to change after all this is over, and your family's too, you just wait and see.'

I felt a wave of embarrassment rise up my chest and I explained that I was blessed already, life was good. 'Anyway, it's all about Mary, not me.'

Rob waved my protests away and fixed me with eyes as clear as rockpools. 'Just you wait, good things are going to come.'

I've never been good with praise, so I changed the subject and launched into my family's geographic history. I explained that my family all came from Texas, a little border town four hours drive south-west of Brisbane. 'We've been in the city a long time now, though. Before that we came from all over: Greece, Germany, Scotland.'

I was trying to be polite, that is, in Aboriginal terms. I had read somewhere that when Aboriginal strangers meet they tell each other which country they belong to and then spend a lot of time figuring out who their common acquaintances are. This process of establishing where you are from and who your people are is terribly important and a nice way of getting comfortable with a person; it certainly seems a lot more civilised than that annoying question we in the white world ask: 'So, what do you do?' Why do we place so much importance on what we *do* rather than who we *are*?

'So, Rob,' I asked, gaining confidence in my first steps in Aboriginal etiquette, 'what's your country?'

Rob broke eye contact and looked away.

I sat frozen as Rob's story wrapped itself around me like a dark vine. This time I couldn't turn the page or switch the channel.

'I was taken from my mother when I was a baby. I've been piecing together my past for a long time now. But on the mission where my clan was sent to, not many records were kept, maybe they didn't want us to remember. I've found most of my relatives now, even in unmarked graves. I also found my mother in 1994; her name is Alma Toomath. We are from Bibbulman country near the sea. Rob's my adopted name, my birth name is Jo Cuttabut. Right now I'm in the process of changing it back to the name my mother gave me.'

Everyone in Australia knows at least a little about the Stolen Generation, about the Aboriginal babies and children who were removed from their mothers, family and culture and placed in government and church-run institutions or with white families. We'll never know the exact numbers of the children whose lives were affected by the removals, which started as far back as 1814 but reached levels of ruthless efficiency from the 1920s until the 1960s. It is estimated that between 10 and 30 per cent of the entire population of Indigenous children were affected by the removal policies. In New South Wales the figure is believed to be up to 10 000 children. In Western Australia, where Rob was born, the figure was even higher. But we'll never know for sure, as records were poor and often destroyed. Comparisons with Nazi Germany are always fraught with danger, but it's worth pointing out that the Nazis kept records in far greater detail of the millions they 'processed' though their death camps during World War II. In fact, a relative or descendant of one of the four million Jews or political prisoners that Hitler exterminated in his death camps stands a better chance of learning the fate of his relatives than an Aboriginal person trying to piece together his or her family history. There is no doubt that some of the motives for the forced removal of children were honourable, but when you read the many stories of the way culture and language were crushed in the institutions, hostels and missions, it is not hard to conclude that the policy was first and foremost an orchestrated program of cultural and spiritual genocide.

It is easy to get disorientated by the many arguments that attempt to justify the government-sanctioned policy of removal; quibbles over percentage points tend to squeeze out the human element of this national tragedy. If you really want to understand, find – and I promise you it won't be difficult – an Indigenous person who has been forcibly removed from the arms of their mother. Sit down in front of him or her and listen to their story. And then make up your own mind.

{ 4 OCTOBER 2005 }

'Hey, I'm comin' up to Brisbane next Wednesday,' Gary announced enthusiastically. 'I'm bringing up a songman too. We'd like to do a proper handover ceremony at your parents' place, nothing big, just a smoking ceremony to clear away any bad spirits and to say thanks.'

'What's a songman?' I asked.

'A cultural man,' said Gary, 'a keeper of our dances and songs.'

A charge of excitement ran through me; all my boyhood Skippy fantasies were about to come true. I smiled like an idiot, picturing two painted-up Aborigines with didgeridoos dancing through smoke on my parents' neatly mown lawn. Then reality shouldered its way back in and I thought of my father; a corroboree in the front yard, it was too weird to contemplate!

'Gary, my dad is a lovely bloke, but I just think that would be too much for him.'

Gary went quiet. I could feel his disappointment and wondered if he was offended.

'Hey, why don't we talk to people at the University,' I suggested. 'That's where it all started.'

Gary liked the idea and suggested that we get some people from the local Indigenous community involved. After the call I buzzed about like a happy fool; then panic set in – I didn't really know anyone in the local Aboriginal community! Mary was about to push me into the unknown, again.

I searched through the University website for Craig's boss, the general manager of the Oodgeroo Unit. It was ten o'clock, but I knew I had to ride the momentum of Gary's call. I punched in the number I'd found and it was answered on the third ring. I was relieved that I hadn't woken Victor up, but he sounded very tired. He explained that he was on Mornington Island as part of a delegation trying to nut out ways to overcome some of the social problems that were tearing up local communities in the region. He patiently and silently listened to my story, just once exclaiming, 'Jee-zus,' when I told him that Mary had spent the last 40 years on my parents' mantelpiece. I told him that two Wamba Wamba men were heading up to Brisbane the following week and were keen to hold a proper handover ceremony at the University. Victor muttered a little and there were lots of deep breaths. And then he thanked me and my family for what we were doing and explained that it was a lot to take in at such a late hour.

'There's a lot of organising to do,' he said. 'These Wamba fellas can't just waltz into town and hold a ceremony without invitation. Our people need to be involved, there are protocols to be observed.'

He explained that he'd had a couple of hard days and promised to get back to me just as soon as he'd digested what I'd told him.

I put down the phone, feeling glad that I'd managed to get the ball rolling, but at the same time feeling as though I'd just assaulted someone. I emailed Gary, again apologising for my father's refusal to meet with him; I wanted Gary to know that Dad was a good man. And then suddenly I thought of football. I'm not sure why, maybe because Gary lived in Victoria, the home of Australian Rules football. My father is a fanatical Essendon supporter – he receives a birthday card from the team each year and has a concrete garden gnome in a red-and-black jumper that he keeps *in* the house because it's so special. At the end of my email I added a little joke, saying, 'Don't hold it against Dad, he's an Essendon supporter, and we know what grumps they can be.'

{ 5 OCTOBER 2005 }

I spread the Horton tribal map of Australia out on the table before my classmates and showed them Mary's country. I was worried that this whole affair was distracting the class, but my lecturer was encouraging and everyone seemed imbued with the 'Let's get Mary home' spirit. After class, I arrived home to find an email from Gary. At the end of his message there was a PS which read, 'By the way, tell your old man that my son plays for the Bombers, number 42. See, we've got something in common after all.' I stared at the email; the only thing missing was the theme music from *The Twilight Zone*.

I phoned Dad and mentioned that there was going to be a handover ceremony at the University and that he and Mum would be most welcome to attend. Dad abruptly declined, saying he had an appointment in town that day. But now I had an ace up my sleeve. As casually as I could, I mentioned Gary's son – number 42. Dad immediately knew who I was talking about.

'That's that young black rookie, Nathan, what's his name—'

'Lovett-Murray,' I added.

'That's it!' Dad always gets excited talking footy. 'He's fast too.'

'Well, Gary is his father, he's the bloke coming up from Victoria to collect Mary. He really wants to meet you, to say thanks.'

There was silence on the phone.

'Anyway, I'll see you soon, Dad.'

Dad just grunted, 'Uhhh,' not in an angry way, but rather as if his mind was elsewhere, as if he had become disoriented.

{ 6 OCTOBER 2005 }

Pete and I have been friends for a long time; he earned the nickname Captain Cranky because he's never afraid to challenge a point of view or to speak his mind. It's an honest friendship! Pete is a mountain-bike race promoter and works from a rustic little shack in his back yard not far from my place. I'd called by to return some tools and had soon settled in for a chat. Pete asked me what I'd been up to, and for the next ten minutes listened – without saying a word – as I told him of Mary's journey back to country. Pete barely batted an eyelid throughout the story, then when I finished he nonchalantly pointed to a rusted old sword hanging above a bookshelf.

'Maybe that's the weapon that did the deed,' he said dryly.

'Pete!' I said, totally appalled. 'Anyway, as if that

dodgy old thing was ever drawn in anger. Where'd you get it, a fancy-dress shop?'

'It's a trooper's sword,' he said.

'So what? It was probably just for ceremonial use.'

'What do you think they used them for, cutting onions for the barbecue?' Pete went on to tell the story behind the sword and how it was given to his father – at the time a fertiliser salesman – by an old farmer.

'The farmer used it as wedge to keep the barn door open. When Dad asked about it the farmer said that it had been there ever since he could remember, but he'd been told it had lopped off a few heads when the land was being cleared.'

Cleared; for some reason I'd always associated the term with trees and scrub. I knew there'd been a few massacres, but I'd imagined that most of the original inhabitants had just drifted away, beyond the ever-expanding line of development. My vivid imagination went into overdrive as I stared at the blunt relic.

'Of course he might have been pulling the old man's leg, you know what farmers are like. He gave it to Dad when he was transferred out of the district.'

'Well, Mary died of syphilis,' I said, for no particular

reason; death by the sword or venereal disease, both were equally horrific ways for body and spirit to part ways.

After my chat with Pete, I thought a lot about white family histories and wondered how many had similar stories, concealed by only a generation or two of dust?

That night Dad phoned. After some smalltalk he asked me about the ceremony; where it was taking place, what time it was to start, how he and Mum could get there. He was playing it cool, and even though I could have leapt down the phone line and planted a kiss on his whiskery cheek, I kept my emotions in check too. He said it was the strangest thing, but in the latest Essendon supporters' magazine there was a three-page article on Nathan Lovett-Murray (Gary's son), and about the Indigenous development program the club runs.

'Gary will be so pleased to meet you and Mum,' I said.

'I look forward to meeting him too,' Dad replied.

The power of football!

CHAPTER EIGHT

{ 7 OCTOBER 2005 }

The handover was only five days away and I was getting jittery. Gary phoned to discuss preparations; he was delighted at the news that Mum and Dad had agreed to come along. Before the call, I'd been reading about the importance Indigenous people place on totems, so I asked Gary what the Wamba Wamba totem was.

'That's a sad story, they're extinct down here now,' he said, and he did sound sad too. 'Our totem's the black cockatoo, the one with the red tail feathers.'

I don't have much hair on my head, but the little bit I have stood on end!

'We call him Wiran,' Gary went on, 'but he's been gone a long time, when the trees were cleared he went too.'

'I saw him, I mean I saw one, last Sunday, on Mount Coot-tha,' I stammered. 'I've never seen one before, and I've been riding through that bush for years.'

'Did he go like this?' Gary asked, his voice bright again. 'Ka-rak, ka-rak!'

'That's him! That's the call! He was looking right at me, calling just like that, he was strong, beautiful—' The words were rushing out of my mouth.

Gary laughed, but he didn't seem at all surprised. 'He was just watching over you, to make sure everything's okay.'

'What, like a guardian?'

'That's it. This is a powerful business, brother, a powerful business. Tell you what, if you can find some of those feathers for the ceremony, it'd be the icing on the cake.' And then he was gone, his parting words – which sounded more like an order than a request – echoing around my head like stones in a tin drum. The phone cord slipped through my hand, each coil passing slowly between my fingers like worry beads until the handset beep-beeped at my feet. Where on earth was I going to find black cockatoo feathers? I pictured myself crawling through the scrub at Mount Coot-tha, and for one silly second considered taking a drive in the country to look for some road-killed crow whose feathers I could doctor with red paint. Maybe the Queensland Museum would lend me one or two; surely they'd have some.

I ran an internet search on black cockatoos and found a scientific journal article on the plight of the species in the southern parts of Australia. The main reason for the bird's disappearance was loss of habitat. Over four million gum trees were chopped down along the Riverine reaches of the Murray River between the mid-1800s and mid-1900s: four million redgums that had provided fruit and nesting hollows for black cockatoos and many other species, sawn into railway sleepers or shipped abroad to shingle the streets of London. Then there were whole forests devastated by the weirs and levees that were constructed all along the Murray, ending the annual floods on which the plains relied for renewal. I scrolled through the article, with its photos, tables and graphs, and there at the end was a colour photograph of a single feather. Then it hit me, of course – the headdress that the Wik women had displayed at the writers festival! I don't know why it took me so long to figure it out. I suppose my mind was overloaded, trying to stay on this weird and wonderful wave that was sweeping Mary homeward. Again I wondered, was the headdress made from the feathers of a black cockatoo, and if it was – and if I could contact the women – would they let me borrow it? It was a week since the festival. Had they returned home to Wik country already?

I knew that one of the women, Fiona, had been published by the same publishing house that had released one of my stories. I looked up my editor's home phone number in the directory. It was a Saturday night and getting late but I decided to throw the dice again before I had the chance to talk myself out of it. I phoned Leonie, and explained rather breathlessly that I needed to get in touch with Fiona and Auntie Alyson. Leonie read out the number in her filofax and explained that Fiona was living in Brisbane and that Auntie Alyson might be still with her. Within a few minutes of remembering the headdress, I had Fiona's phone number in my hand.

Fiona was having a pleasant evening with her family in front of the television when I phoned her. I introduced myself and explained that I had attended her talk at the writers festival and told her how I had been mesmerised by the headdress. Then I mentioned that I had grown up with an Aboriginal skull on my family mantelpiece. She groaned, as though I had reached down the telephone line and punched her in the stomach. Her reaction must have alarmed her family because the volume of the television in the background suddenly dropped and I heard a concerned voice ask, 'What's wrong?' I continued, Fiona punctuating my story with gasps and exclamations of bewilderment. I felt as though I was bludgeoning her. I finished my story by going through all of the coincidences: the black cockatoo at Mount Coot-tha, the headdress, the lost Wamba Wamba totem and Gary's request that I find some feathers. There was a long silence, and then she said, 'So, are you asking me if you can borrow the headdress?'

'Fiona,' I stammered, 'I'm not sure why I'm talking to you, I'm not even sure they are the right feathers, and I don't even know if they're yours – I suppose Auntie Alyson has taken them back to Wik country.'

'My sister has gone, but the headdress is mine, I'm looking at it right now.' Her voice was measured and calm. There was a short silence before she continued, 'And because you have told me this story, I am obliged to let you have the headdress. When would you like to collect it?'

{ 9 OCTOBER 2005 }

Fiona lived on the far side of Brisbane, across the river which divides the city and close enough to Moreton Bay to smell the ocean. My four-year-old-daughter Bianca was in the car with me. I was a nervous wreck and I suppose I took Bianca along as a security blanket; to demonstrate that I was a good father and not the skull-cradling ghoul I felt like. I was too uptight to consult the street directory; I knew where the suburb was and for some unfathomable reason I imagined that my own intuition would lead me to the correct street. I became hopelessly lost, and even after checking the directory I overshot the turnoff to Fiona's street by kilometres. I suppose I was nervous about stepping through the door of an Aboriginal home for the first time in my life. Would it be a rundown place with broken windows and a yard full of car bodies and yapping dogs, the classic media cliché that's rolled out every other night on television? But no, that wouldn't have worried me; I knew that Fiona was a strong and gifted woman, a fellow writer, a dancer and actor. I wouldn't have cared if she'd lived in a tent. Perhaps *that* was what I was afraid of, meeting an Indigenous woman who positively radiated her culture, a culture that mine had endeavoured to keep under its heel for the last 200 years.

When I scribbled down the street name Fiona had given me – Cook Street – I hadn't given it any thought. But as I got closer I noticed that all the surrounding streets bore the names of famous British explorers: Wentworth, Blaxland, Cunningham, Leichhardt; men whose expeditions opened the country up to waves of settlers who in turn pushed the original inhabitants from their homelands. Fiona's home was halfway down Cook Street – named after the legendary English seafarer who'd claimed her ancestors' country for the British Empire. And just in case anyone missed the obvious connection, her street was flanked by signposts which read James, Endeavour and Banks. For the first time in my life I felt the power of name, what it must be like to be constantly reminded – even in subtle and unintentional ways like this – that your land has been conquered, and that you, a descendant of the original owners, are now part of a minority, an 'Other'. I wondered if Fiona felt a pang of discomfort or resentment whenever she wrote out her address, or was she used to it. I decided not to ask; I'd stepped on enough sensibilities lately.

Bianca and I pulled into the driveway of a neat little brick house. Why did I make the mental note that it was *neat*? Had my conditioning been so thorough that anything other than a clapped-out, corrugated-iron cliché would come as a surprise? Had the media done that good a job on me? Good god, was I carrying around some baggage!

Fiona's two youngest daughters spilled out of the house; they held back for a moment, trying to look shy, but once they saw Bianca their smiles lit up like sunbeams. Fiona followed, looking a little hesitant, but after sizing me up for a moment invited us in. Inside the lounge room it was all perfectly 'normal': *Australia's Funniest Home Videos* was playing softly on the television set, Fiona's eldest daughter gossiped to a friend on the phone, a computer workstation sat in a corner overflowing with folders. But there was a strong cultural presence here too: the walls were covered with Indigenous paintings and prints, Aboriginal handicrafts and books dotted the bookshelves, and family smiled proudly in traditional dress from framed photographs. Everywhere the colours of the land dominated – natural yellows, ochres, reds – colours of country that brought the outside inside. It was much more than *neat*; here was a home that straddled two worlds. And there, high on the bookshelf, was perched the black cockatoo headdress.

Fiona's husband, Danny, was working through a set of vigorous exercises and stretches on the floor. I sat on the couch with Bianca beside me and tried to look relaxed. Danny jumped up and shook my hand – hard! – before launching himself into another set of stretches. This man was well put together, and as his muscles rippled the word 'warrior' flashed through my head. I asked Danny whether he boxed, tilting my head towards a picture of Anthony Mundine on the wall. He shook his head and explained that he'd just set up a personal training business. 'It's gunna be a growth industry, you just wait and see; got a few steady clients already.'

Fiona's younger daughter Ebony, who had been holding back, was unable to contain herself any longer.

She leapt in front of Bianca with her hands out. 'Let's play!' Bianca flew off the couch and the two skipped down the hallway to Ebony's room.

'Tell me your story again,' Fiona asked. 'Danny!' she gently remonstrated as her husband began another impressive set of contortions.

'Don't mind him,' she smiled. I could tell by the way she looked at her husband that she was crazy about him. He shot her a cheeky grin back.

I told the story again, in more detail than I'd told her over the phone. Every now and then she winced in pain or shook her head.

'I'm sorry,' she said, 'I just find this so hard to comprehend – I mean, why?' She turned to Danny. 'Can you imagine having a whitefella's skull on our mantelpiece?'

Danny was glistening with a light coat of sweat, the veins in his arms bulged and I was expecting at any moment to be thrown out the door for upsetting his wife. When I got to the end of the story – to the bit about the cockatoo – Danny took down the headdress, gently stroking and straightening the feathers as Fiona explained the importance of birds.

'They're our messengers. Just the other day one landed on my windowsill and straight away I knew an auntie was sick. I rang her up and sure enough she had a really bad stomach bug.'

'This is beeswax,' Danny explained, pointing to the black, resin-like lump that held the feathers in place. 'It's strong stuff, but this headdress has been travelling to lots of dances, so it's getting a bit knocked around.'

He placed the headdress in my lap.

'Don't worry, I'll take good care of it,' I promised.

Danny pointed to one of the feathers. 'This one's broken, I've just put some Blu-Tack behind it to keep it straight.'

Giggles and laughter wafted up the hallway from Ebony's room and washed over us. I felt much more at ease, with the laughter, with the headdress in my lap.

'Is it always like this?' I asked Fiona.

'What do you mean?' she said.

'Well, *this*, this thing that's happening, this power. It feels as though Mary's being carried home on a wave that just keeps building. I feel as though I'm hanging on moment by moment.'

'That's the way life is supposed to be,' said Fiona.

'It's normal for us, the land is telling us things all the time.'

And then she said something that I will carry with me forever. 'You're just a whitefella who's learnt to listen, that's all.'

Ebony and Bianca came bounding into the lounge room.

'Look, Dad, look what Ebony gave me!' Bianca held up her wrist. Around it was wrapped a homemade bracelet with Ebony's name spelt out in beads.

Fiona smiled. 'Trading gifts already!'

If not for the difference in colour, our two girls could have been twins; their hair was the same length and they even wore similar flowing dresses.

'Bianca is an Italian name,' I said, 'it means white. Ebony and Bianca, black and white.' There were smiles all around, until I put my foot in it. I must have gotten carried away by all the lovin' in the room.

'Ebony's a special name in our house, we have a big, fat black chook called Ebony.'

Suddenly all that lovin' froze.

Fiona wasn't sure what to say. 'You have a black chicken called Ebony?'

'She's more like one of the family,' I said meekly.

'She's beautiful,' beamed Bianca.

Fiona shook her head and laughed.

As if on cue, we all rose and headed for the door. I placed the headdress gently into the back seat and said goodbye, promising to return the feathers in a weeks time.

Just before bedtime the phone rang. It was Bob Weatherall, the repatriation expert who had been away fishing. He had a voice as smooth and as deep as the river bend I imagined he'd been camping at; and when he laughed, it was with the lightness of a songbird. He'd received my message and had also heard about the handover on the grapevine. Bob explained that he was getting things organised and suggested we touch base again the next day. He was completely calm and relaxed, the way you'd expect someone to sound after spending two weeks fishing in country that they loved. He told me that he and his mate had snuck into a good fishing spot on a neighbouring clan's land without asking for permission.

'There we were, lines in the water, out in the middle of nowhere, and suddenly this *old* fella comes out from the reeds waggin' his finger at us like we were two naughty boys. I said, "You got us, Uncle, you got us!" He laughed with that sing-songy hee-hee laugh of his. It was a laugh that told me Mary was in safe hands.

CHAPTER NINE

{ 10 OCTOBER 2005 }

I rode to the suburban campus of the University early
in the morning, the gravel crackling beneath my tyres
as I followed a bush track that ran through a reserve.
I looked for black cockatoos, but instead had to contend
with a squealing, wheeling rainbow of nectar-drunk
lorikeets. One defecated in mid-flight, its quicksilver
poop catching the morning sun.

My first lecture of the day wasn't due to start for an
hour, so I headed for Craig's office at the Oodgeroo

Unit. Craig was sitting rigidly at attention with the phone pressed to his ear. He waved me in, motioned to a chair and mouthed the word 'Victor'. I could hear the raised voice of Craig's boss barking a continual stream of instructions down the line.

'He just came in two seconds ago.' Craig passed me the handset and slumped back; his office chair reclined with a groan.

Victor's voice seemed to have lowered a notch or two when he spoke to me, but not much; he explained that he was quite stressed from the Mornington Island business and that the timing of the handover couldn't be worse for the unit, though he understood that the reburial couldn't be postponed.

'Everything has to be done correctly, a whitefella can't just invite Wamba Wamba fellas up here to perform a ceremony in Turrbal Country, otherwise it's just terra bloody nullius all over again.'

'Sorry, you've lost me, what's *terrible* country?' I asked.

'*Turrbal*! *Turrbal* country; Brisbane; where you're sitting right now.' He let go a frustrated sigh. 'Look, we'll make sure the old fella gets sent home properly, but if it's not done correctly there'll be a lot of elders lining up to kick my arse and this unit cannot afford to have its arse kicked.'

I handed the phone back to Craig and heard Victor's voice go back up to its previous levels. Craig simply said, 'Yes, yes, I understand, yes, don't worry, got it, yes.'

My post-ride afterglow was a rapidly fading memory.

Craig put down the smoking handset, collapsed back into his reclining office chair and exhaled.

'Sorry,' I offered pathetically.

'Don't worry about it. You've done the right thing. It gets a bit complicated around Brisbane, we don't just have to get permission from the Turrbal clan, we have to inform the Jugera group as well.'

Craig explained that the Turrbal clan was virtually wiped out when Brisbane was settled, which opened the door for other groups, mainly the Jugera, to claim the Brisbane area as their ancestral homeland.

'These things can get a bit political; plenty of our own people are just waiting to jump on us if they think we're stepping out of line.'

I'd once read that Aboriginal tribes required permission to travel across the country of others, but

I'd never considered that these same laws and territorial protocols might still be in place today.

'When one clan carries out business, any business, in another clan's country, there has to be discussion, consultation, permission,' Craig explained, 'especially with Sorry Business. That's the most serious business of all.'

{ 11 OCTOBER 2005 }

Next morning I visited the main office of the Oodgeroo Unit, at the University's inner-city campus. This was the unit's headquarters, four times as big as the suburban campus's office I had visited the day before. I had scurried past its glass doors and courtyard many times, but this was my first ever visit inside. At the front desk, a pretty young woman called Katie looked up from her work and smiled.

'Hi, my name's John, I'm involved in tomorrow's handover ceremony.'

Katie's eyes widened. 'We were only told this morning, can you believe this family *actually* kept a skull in their lounge room.'

'Yes, I can.' I felt totally naked. 'That was my family, I'm the fella handing it back.'

Katie looked at me – into me – but there was no judgement or negativity in her eyes.

'Your family is doing the right thing, but I tell you, everyone here's in a flap with Victor away and all these people coming tomorrow. It's the first time we've ever done anything like this.'

Katie directed me outside to the courtyard where the acting manager was briefing the campus building managers and heads of security. Victor's stand-in was a slight woman in her late fifties, but her voice packed the punch of a school headmistress and the men she briefed listened attentively. I moved to the side of the courtyard, sat under the shade of a tree and listened in. What an ants' nest I'd stirred up! The air-conditioning plant for the entire block needed to be shut down because the intake ducts were near where the smoking ceremony was to take place. The fire and safety wardens of all the surrounding blocks were to be informed to prevent any panic once the smoke started billowing. Extra security staff had to be posted at strategic points to keep curious onlookers at bay, and the Indigenous members of the security department needed to be informed about the Sorry Business so that they could choose either to become involved, or to avoid the area altogether. Concrete table and chair settings had to be moved from the courtyard by a heavy lifting vehicle, and replaced with rows of single plastic chairs. The list went on and on. The manager hadn't noticed me, so I slunk away, embarrassed, overwhelmed. It was a ten-minute walk to where my car was parked; halfway there I stopped, took a few deep breaths, and headed back to face the music.

The Oodgeroo Unit courtyard was now empty of officials; two staff on tea break puffed cigarettes. As I walked past I caught a fragment of their quiet conversation that I'm sure included the word 'skull'.

'Oh there you are,' said Katie as I re-entered the office. 'We were wondering where you'd got to.'

She led me into the acting manager's office where I was greeted with a generous smile. I began to apologise for all the disruption I'd caused, but the acting manager waved my words away. She was more concerned with how I was coping! She handed me a running sheet for the next day's ceremony and asked me to check with the Wamba Wamba people that everything was in accordance with their wishes. 'Don't you worry about a thing,' she smiled, 'it's going to be a beautiful handover.'

I spent the rest of the day at home working the phone – I'd never spent so much time on the phone as I had in these last two weeks! Emails bounced backwards and forwards. Gary gave the running sheet the thumbs-up. The University media unit swung into action and together we worked up a press release which was then wired out to media outlets all around the country. Within minutes of the press release going out, the local ABC radio station had requested an interview at the station in the morning with Bob, Gary and me.

That evening I called Bob to let him know about the interview. He was happy to have an opportunity to speak about repatriation. 'We have to use these opportunities to educate the people, it's all part of the healing.'

I offered to pick Bob up early in the morning, for it made sense to go to the radio station together; we'd meet Gary and the songman for the interview and then all head off for the ceremony.

'If the songman's with Gary, will you have enough room for everybody?' he asked.

'Sure,' I answered, 'I'll just put the remains in the boot.'

'You'll what?' Bob's words came out in one even sound, like a samurai sword being slowly drawn from its scabbard.

I suddenly realised that by *everybody* Bob was also referring to Mary.

'Uh, oh, ahhh . . .' I'd put my foot in it again. 'Sorry, Bob, I wasn't thinking, yes, there'll be room for us all up front.'

'That's more like it,' he said, the warmth ebbing back into his voice. 'See you at 7.30.'

Mary lay in my studio under the house. Since bringing him home, I'd kept him in a hard black Pelican case – the kind photographers use – with the cockatoo feather headdress sitting on top like a sentinel. With careful hands I put the headdress to one side, took Mary out and wandered into the back yard. The moon was shining through the canopy of native trees I'd planted when we moved in ten years ago. It was very late and the neighbouring houses were all dark and still. I held Mary towards the moon and whispered, 'This is it, Mary, your last night in Meanjin.' (Meanjin is the traditional name for Brisbane.)

We stood near my favourite tree, an eight-year-old
lemon-scented myrtle. A breeze wafted up from the
gully and through the tree, bathing us both in citrus
perfume. I'd been wondering what to wrap Mary in for
her journey home – bubble wrap seemed so twenty-
first century. Now I knew. I took Mary back inside
and returned to the tree; thick waves of citrus filled
the night as I snapped and tore off armfuls of foliage.
I made a bed of leaves and sprigs in the case and sat
Mary upright with the headdress propped up behind
him against the open lid – it looked as though he was
wearing it. Then I placed the whole arrangement near
the window; I'm not exactly sure why, I didn't think,
I just acted naturally, like a child. I switched off the
lights, and then, just before leaving the room, turned to
look back at my old friend. Moonlight spilled through
the window and draped its lacy veil across Mary and
the headdress.

CHAPTER
TEN

{ 12 OCTOBER 2005 }

Just after sun-up, the songman phoned. It was Jason, the young man I'd spoken to when I'd first made contact with Mary's people; he had arrived – without Gary! There had been another death in the clan and Gary was obliged to stay behind in Melbourne to take care of the arrangements. It seemed that every second time I spoke with an Aboriginal person, someone close to them had died.

'Another one!' I spat the words out. It makes me cringe now to admit it, but I felt very put out; I might as well have said, 'Can't you people stop dying, we're trying to organise a repatriation here!'

'Yeah, we've had a bad run lately; we've lost four in the last few weeks.'

'I'm sorry,' I said, trying to sound sympathetic, and I was, but the news of Gary's non-arrival had knocked the wind out of me.

'Listen, John, I can hear you're disappointed, but we're going to do this, and it's going be fine, okay.'

The confidence in Jason's voice reassured me. He was right; Mary was still going home and that's all that mattered. We agreed to meet at the ABC Radio studios at 9 a.m.

'Why is Daddy staring so hard at nothing?' Bianca asked.

'Don't forget to chew,' said Stella as I gulped down the bacon-and-egg breakfast she'd prepared. 'You won't be of use to anyone if you choke.'

It was true, my mind was far away and I was forking food into my maw as if I was shovelling coal into a furnace. After breakfast I spent a few minutes touching up a short speech that I'd been wrestling with; somehow the short speech had ballooned into six pages. There was a long list of people to thank and acknowledge, but more importantly, how could I possibly explain the bizarre relationship between my family and a long-deceased Wamba Wamba man? The more I wrote the more knotted up I became, until I realised that what I was really doing was trying to justify a wrongdoing. With a heavy black marker I crossed out line upon line, until only a third of the speech remained. I folded the pages and put them in my pocket. I'd have another look at it later, now it was time to pack Mary.

I opened the studio door, and the scent of lemon myrtle greeted me – the room, the case, everything smelt clean, renewed. I laid Mary on his side and packed the leaves around him tightly; he looked majestic wrapped in his green going-away finery. I tried to say something poignant but realised that the night before had been our proper farewell – the moon, the dancing trees, the silence had said it all. The case catches closed with a final farewell snap. The fragrance lingered on my fingers; I put them to my nose and inhaled deeply, feeling myself relax a little. I followed my feet out into the yard and tore some larger branches from the lemon myrtle. My feet then took me to the garage where our little blue

Mazda hatchback sat. I brushed the branches through the car's interior, purifying it, and then arranged them neatly along the back parcel shelf, pushing the sprigs flat so I'd be able to see out the rear window. Gathering up the loose leaves, I tore them into smaller pieces and jammed the native potpourri into the ashtray; I hoped Bob and Jason weren't smokers – if they were we'd be having our own little ceremonial fire in the Mazda! I had no idea what I was doing, I was letting instinct lead me. When I'd finished, the car reminded me of a funeral boat, the sort that took fallen Nordic warriors across the misty waters to Valhalla.

I kissed Stella and my two daughters; they were going to meet me at the ceremony later. I was worried the girls might freak out from all the noise and whatever it was that the songman had planned. 'Now, there's going to be loud didgeridoo music and dancing and smoke, but there's nothing to be scared of, Grandma and Grandad will be there too.'

'Will it be a party, Daddy?' asked Bianca.

Two-year-old Lydia looked up expectantly. 'Cake!'

I opened my mouth to say no, but nothing came out.

'Daddy doesn't know, sweetie,' Stella answered, 'it's

going to be an adventure for all of us.'

I placed Mary's case and the headdress on the front seat, buckled him in, and drove off to get Bob.

Bob's house was a simple postwar cottage, similar to many others in the street except there was no front fence, just a big mango tree and grass that spilled out to the footpath. I like yards without fences. A friend of mine has an Italian father-in-law who often observes, 'When I first came to this country, the fences were this big' (he indicates by putting his hand at waist height) 'and everybody happy. Now the fences all this big' (he says, holding his hand over his head) 'and nobody happy.'

I climbed the few short steps and knocked – the door was open. The front room looked like an office; a tall filing cabinet adorned with Aboriginal pride and activism stickers blocked most of my view. A computer hummed away in the background while piles of folders leaned this way and that. It was the sort of workspace where the in-tray never emptied.

'See you this afternoon, love,' Bob called over his shoulder as he came to the door.

I recognised his face instantly from the years of

television and newspaper stories on Aboriginal affairs and activism; stories that my father had snorted at, stories that I had ignored. He held out his hand. Bob had a smoky beard the size of Santa's but without the curly bits. He wore a bushman's hat, boots and jeans. A screenprint of a fierce Mayan figure stretched across his black T-shirt; underneath, the words read 'World Congress of Indigenous Peoples'. I guessed that Bob was in his late fifties or early sixties, but the mischievous twinkle in his eye made it hard to tell. I could picture him as a cute ten-year-old getting his plump cheeks squeezed by a gaggle of adoring aunties.

'Where's Gary?' he asked, noticing the empty car.

'Not coming. Death in the clan,' I explained. 'But Jason arrived this morning, we're meeting him at the radio station.'

Bob stopped mid-step, pausing to digest the information.

'Okay,' he said in a tone of total acceptance. 'Let's go.'

Mary lay in the front seat.

'Where would you like to ride?' I asked.

Bob paused again for a few moments. 'I'll ride up front, put him behind me.'

I moved Mary to the rear seat and strapped him back in.

Bob climbed into the front then reached around and very gently patted and rubbed the top of the case. 'How you going, old man?' he asked quietly.

We drove off.

'You would've been better off going the other way,' Bob advised as we headed down his street.

I stopped and crunched the car into reverse. After a couple of hundred metres we had gathered speed and the Mazda's differential started to protest. Bob asked casually, almost gently so as not to distract my reverse driving concentration, 'Ever heard of a U-turn?'

'I was just going to back into that side street back there but I missed it,' I explained. 'I'll get the next one.'

'That's good,' he said, 'thought you might be reversing all the way into town.'

I continued to reverse. A car approached us from behind, travelling the right way. It began flashing its lights. I reversed into the side street with only a metre or two to spare. Bob slammed his foot into an imaginary brake pedal and began muttering something about the sweet mother of god.

Bee-eeeeeep!!!! The car swept by, its driver waving his fist through the window.

I looked at Bob; he was a lot paler than when he'd first climbed aboard. He adjusted his hat and I apologised. 'I'm a bit nervous.'

'So am I!' he answered.

Although Bob's foot continued to hit his imaginary brake pedal and I noticed that his fingers had assumed a python-like grip on the armrest, we arrived at the ABC studios without further incident. It wasn't *just* my driving, he reassured me, city traffic always made him nervous. Bob disappeared for a nerve-settling smoke while I spoke to the security lady on the gate. She found my name on the visitors list and gave me two nametags.

'I've got you down as three visitors, possibly four?'

'No, just the one more,' I explained. 'Keep an eye out for a lost-looking Aboriginal guy with a didgeridoo.'

Moments later a yellow taxi glided up to the gate; the driver and the passenger sat for a while, winding up a conversation as the motor idled. Eventually the cab door opened and laughter poured out, followed by Jason Tamiru, the hippest, strongest, friendliest-looking Aboriginal man I had ever seen.

'He doesn't look lost to me!' cooed the woman from the security booth, her appreciative eyes running up and down Jason's impressive frame.

The cab driver helped Jason get his didgeridoo and bags from the back of the station wagon. In fact he was the most helpful and pleasant cabbie I think I've ever seen. He seemed smitten with Jason and looked as though he wanted to come to the interview with us!

The interview was to be pre-recorded and would go to air later that day. Bob, Jason and I sat on one side of the booth and the interviewer sat on the other. After a really nice introduction the announcer went straight for the freak-show angle.

'So, John, tell us, what's it like growing up with a skull in the family living room?'

A little wave of anger swept up my spine. This was my family we were talking about in public. I took a deep breath and explained my father's eclectic collection and pointed out that Mary was not a trophy. I surprised myself by how clearly and purposefully I spoke. Thankfully the rest of the interview centred on the true spirit of the story: Mary's journey home. Bob was an old hand when it came to working the media. He spoke clearly and precisely, explaining how human remains had been plundered from burial sites through the 1800s and 1900s and shipped by the crateload to local and overseas institutions for scientific study. He explained that while many colleges, universities and museums were starting to return remains from their collections, about 10 000 were still held by Australian institutions and 5000 by their British counterparts. However, these figures represented only the numbers that repatriation experts had been able to accurately confirm.

'Even today,' Bob explained, 'collectors and antique dealers are quietly trading the remains of our ancestors on the internet. But the overwhelming majority sit in cardboard boxes and plastic bags in museum basements and dungeons all around the world.'

The interviewer asked the question my father had asked. 'Bob, a lot of people will be listening, thinking, what's the big deal? You don't know who it is, it's possibly thousands of years old, why worry about it?'

'The dead have rights,' replied Bob firmly. 'They have the right to be placed in their final resting place, in their own country, so that they can enter the spirit world and become one with their mother, the Earth.'

But the interview wasn't all serious and sombre.

It ended with the story about my father's reluctance to attend the ceremony until he learned that Gary's son played for his beloved Essendon Football Club. Everyone fell about the booth in hysterics when I mentioned Dad's Essendon garden gnome, attired in the black-and-red jersey with a little football tucked under his arm. There was lots of laughter and ribbing – it was a nice way to finish up.

Out in the carpark, we handed in our security passes. The security officer was still all eyes for Jason – this guy had magnetism! Ten o'clock; we had just over an hour to get to the ceremony. The University was only a ten-minute drive away, so we had plenty of time.

'Nice headdress,' said Jason as he climbed into the back seat beside Mary. His nose twitched, following the scent of citrus to the parcel shelf behind him. 'Hey, I love this stuff!' He ran his hand through the bushy arrangement and put his fingers to his nose. 'Makes wicked tea, and you can cook with it too, it's great for smoking fish.'

'What's that?' asked Bob from the front, half twisting to see what Jason was talking about but keeping one eye firmly on the road.

'All this lemon myrtle back here, what's its botanical

name, Citra-something?'

'*Backhousia citriodora,*' I said, hoping I wasn't sounding like a know-all.

Bob nodded his approval and got back to the important business of scrutinising my driving.

Jason and Bob hadn't had a chance to say much to each other prior to the interview; now they fired off the names of family and acquaintances, teasing out shared connections and the corresponding root notes of their personal and tribal songlines. As each common relationship was established, they relaxed – quite visibly – into each other's company. I felt privileged to listen in as the two men exchanged news and gossip that, quite literally, traversed the continent. As it turned out, Jason wasn't from Wamba Wamba country at all, he was a Yorta Yorta man. However, as the clans were close neighbours and as Jason was a nephew of Gary's, he possessed both the knowledge and the connections required to receive Mary and to escort him back to country.

Just as we were about to turn left onto the main feeder road that led to the University, Bob called out, 'Hang a right at the bridge up here, we've just got to pick up a coolamon from West End.'

In an instant we were crossing the river and heading in the opposite direction. I looked at my watch; an hour to go, we'd be okay. Every now and then Bob would interrupt the conversation to call out, 'Right, left, up this way, down here,' all the while punctuating his directions with involuntary thumps to the floor with his brake-pedal foot. What a sight we must have made: a super-cool hugely Afro'd Yorta Yorta songman, a jittery, bearded Kamilaroi man, a balding white chauffeur, a didgeridoo, a feather headdress, half a forest and a mysterious black case, all crammed into a blue Mazda hatchback.

'Here it is, whoa, brother, in here!' called Bob.

I hit the brakes hard; the delivery truck on our tail tooted in protest as Bob muttered a few more choice words about the holy mother.

Loose bitumen crunched under our tyres as we climbed the narrow service road that snaked into Musgrave Park. Apart from the occasional music and cultural festival, Musgrave Park isn't generally frequented by too many white folk. An Aboriginal meeting and ceremonial place for thousands of years before settlement, and for almost 200 years an epicentre of Indigenous resistance, this was the place where

Brisbane blacks drew a line in the sand and said, 'This is ours.' I'd always thought of Musgrave Park as a no-go zone, a place where Indigenous locals gathered to obliterate their brain cells with cask wine, solvent fumes and fists. So it was a surprise for me to find a cultural centre tucked away in the park. Three older fellows lounged on the railing of the prim little weatherboard hall; they were snappily dressed in the way that people who grew up in the 1940s and 1950s tend to dress – in high trousers, collared shirts and felt trilby hats. They greeted us all warmly and shot the breeze with Bob for a while. The centre was staffed by a couple of older ladies who greeted us like long-lost friends when we entered. There was something so genuine about these people; they possessed an unhurried generosity of spirit that now seems so rare – so endangered – in twenty-first-century Australia.

Bob asked the ladies if he could borrow a coolamon for the smoking ceremony. The ladies poked about the office, behind boxes, on top of filing cabinets.

'Sorry, dear, someone must have borrowed it,' said one with a shrug and a smile.

As Bob and Jason talked over the coolamon situation, one of the ladies approached me. 'Where are you from, love?' she asked with a face that radiated pure grandmotherly love.

'My family's all from Texas, but we live in Brisbane now,' I said, and then added quietly, 'What's a coolamon?'

'It's a wooden bowl,' she said, elegantly conjuring a long, shallow shape in the air with her hands.

I felt quite privileged to be in that place with those people, even if it was only for a few minutes. Musgrave Park proved the perfect metaphor for my experiences over the last two weeks. Here was this place that from the outside seemed so intimidating, so poisoned by bad press; Mary had forced me to push through the skin of negativity (and what a deceptively thin skin it was!) to the rich and welcoming cultural centre that awaited.

The warm, fuzzy interlude was soon shattered when I heard Bob announce, 'No worries, I'll just make one.'

'Make one!' I thought, looking at my watch. The ceremony was due to start in 45 minutes.

We drove back down the service road. My two companions were having a chuckle about something when two drunken or drugged Aboriginal men crashed out of the bushes and lurched across the road in front of us. One of the rubber men paused, his unsteady eyes fixed on me for a moment; in them I saw his bewildered spirit entombed in bloodshot madness.

'Don't run over the drones,' said Bob in that samurai-sword voice of his. He shook his head and uttered a few more choice words, but beneath his anger I noticed a hint of embarrassment. For some reason, Bob's reaction to the drunks surprised me. I suppose I'd naively thought that Aboriginal people were one big club, one big mind united in the struggle. I was fast learning their society was just like any other, with its own hierarchy of politicians and poets, jokers and brooders, winners and wastrels.

Bob's good humour returned when we hit the streets again. 'What we need is a good paperbark tree; keep your eyes peeled, boys.'

'Are you sure you've got time to make a bowl?' I said, nervously pointing at the dashboard clock. 'I could swing by my place and pick something up, would a wok do the trick?'

Bob and Jason rolled about laughing.

'Relax, brother!' Jason said, leaning forward to slap me on the shoulder, 'you're running on Nunga time now.'

Bob laughed in that little bird way of his. 'Tee-hee-hee. They can't really start without us, can they?'

We must have taken the most indirect route possible to the University. We never seemed to travel in a straight line for more than 50 metres. 'Over there, brother. No, try up this street.' Every time I looked in the rear-view mirror it was filled by Jason's big, laughing face. No one could have guessed we were on our way to a solemn ceremony.

'Quick, hang a U-turn, I think I see some paper-barks over there,' ordered Bob.

I turned the car hard; one of the wheels caught the median strip, lurching the driver's side of the car into the air. Bob stomped on his imaginary brake pedal as his hat and beard became airborne. After he'd caught his breath he turned to me and said, 'Geez, you only clipped it, brother, turn around and have another crack at it, you might kill it this time!'

Tears of laughter streamed down my cheeks; Bob made a show of straightening his beard and hat while Jason's baritone laugh bounced about the cabin.

'Here we go, stop here! Look, there's a whole clump of them,' said Bob, pointing to a dozen or so paperbarks.

We were on a busy six-lane road festooned with CLEARWAY and NO STOPPING signs.

'I can't stop here!' I protested as I pulled into the bus-only lane and slowed down.

'We'll only be a second – if the law comes, tell 'em we're on sacred business,' advised Bob as he leapt from the car.

Bob and Jason laughed like young boys on an emu chase as they sprinted across the park to the trees. The two men studied a few trees and exchanged opinions before Bob pointed to the one he thought was best. I watched in disbelief as he wrapped his arms around the tree and shimmied up the trunk a metre or two like a koala, then pulled until the bark began to come away. He let himself fall to the ground and as he came down a great section of bark came down with him. He and Jason jogged back to the car with a section of paperbark about the size of a small surfboard.

We had our smoking bowl.

CHAPTER
ELEVEN

A parking space had been set aside for us at the suburban campus. As the heat from the engine block tick-ticked away, so did the frivolity and humour that had filled the car for the last hour. We must have looked as though we meant business; Jason with his mysterious dufflebag in one hand and his didgeridoo case balanced on his shoulder; Bob with his cowboy hat pulled down low and the enormous slab of paperbark under his arm; and me with the headdress in one hand and my black case in the other. We strode with purpose; we were Mary's minions now, doing the earthly things required to get his waylaid soul back to the spirit world. We were being reeled in. Our path seemed energised, lit up like a runway that only we could see; the throngs and gaggles of people on everyday university business parted before us.

'Here they come, here they come.' A rustling of whispers rose in intensity as we passed through the Oodgeroo Unit courtyard. Somehow we had managed to arrive a few minutes early, but already clusters of people milled around, looking at us while trying not to, eyes scanning each of us before coming to rest on the black case. Inside the Unit offices, the mostly female staff flitted about, trying in vain to look focused, as if it was business as usual, but there was a still, twittery tension, the way a forest feels when stormclouds boil across the hilltops and the tempest is about to hit.

Craig rushed towards us. 'You're here! We were starting to worry. This way, Victor's still away, you can use his room, where's Gary?'

He ushered us into his boss's office. Craig and Bob knew each other; I introduced him to Jason and the two made smalltalk before Craig pulled me aside.

'Mate,' he whispered, ' I've got to tell you, some of my staff are really upset.'

'Why, what's happened?' I asked, fearing I'd made another cultural blunder.

'They're sick, physically and emotionally,' he pointed to his heart. 'This is *bad* business, and some of them just can't deal with it – it's too strong. They want to know if it's going to be visible.'

I must have looked at him with a gormless expression.

'The remains!' he whispered loudly. 'Are you taking them out of the case, are we going to *see* the skull?'

'Oh no. Of course not!' I assured Craig that Mary wouldn't be making an appearance; he'd be staying in the case and we wouldn't even be seeing that. 'Your flag will be draped over the whole thing.'

Craig's body relaxed a little. 'I'm sorry, Victor's left me in charge and if anything goes wrong I'll be getting my arse kicked till this time next year.'

'You know, Craig, it's weird, but it's almost as if Mary's chosen us,' I explained in a rare moment of lucidity. 'Victor's away, Gary couldn't make it, my dad won't personally hand the remains back; instead it's you, Jason and me – a younger generation has been asked to step up. And we *can* do this, it'll be fine.'

I don't know where the words came from, but they made Craig and me feel a little calmer.

I returned to the office, where Bob and Jason were sitting silently. It was well past eleven o'clock now. The three of us sat together for a few minutes; hardly a word was exchanged. Finally, Jason got to his feet and announced, 'Fellas, I need to paint up and get myself ready.'

We left the Yorta Yorta songman and Mary and headed through the office towards the courtyard. It was difficult to walk more than a few steps without someone asking a question, wanting to know what was happening, wanting to know what the plan was. Out in the courtyard people were gathering at the perimeter of a circle half made up of chairs, half imagined; in the centre stood a lone table. An area had been set for the media contingent, who busied themselves unfolding tripods, unwinding cables and checking over camera equipment. A blur of Indigenous faces – people who introduced themselves, touched me, and asked if I was okay. I was taken aback; I was the representative of a family that had violated the dead, yet everyone I spoke to was genuinely concerned for *my* wellbeing!

Usually it is the coloured faces that stand out in a crowd. Today it was the turn of the white ones; my lecturers and fellow students all floated in stark relief amid the sea of brown skin and dark curls.

My parents – I'd forgotten them! Big Rob was easy to find, he towered above the other guests; I asked him if he could take my family under his wing when they arrived.

'They got here ages ago, some of the ladies are looking after them in the lunchroom,' he said, pointing to a set of glass doors at the far end of the courtyard. I poked my head in to make sure they were okay. A blur, a swirling blur, so many people. Bob Weatherall looked serene, as if this was what he had been born to do. He patted me on the shoulder and gestured to the trees that lined the narrow courtyard. 'Paperbarks,' he smiled, 'good ones too.' He took his bark coolamon to a nearby tap and let water run over it, massaging the moisture into the layers of pulpy fibre so that it wouldn't catch fire.

A newspaper reporter cruised up to my side like a shark. 'You're John, right? Listen, I've only allowed half an hour for this job and you're running late, so what I'd like to do is set up a quick photo of you and that

Aboriginal fella holding the skull – with maybe the fire and the flag in the background.'

'No. We can't do that,' I replied, not quite believing what I'd just heard. My mind leapt back 20 years; I'd just left school and wasn't sure what to do with my life and Dad had gone berserk when I mentioned that I might like to be a journalist. Now I understood why.

'Well, can we just snap a few photographs of the skull, it'll take thirty seconds?'

I opened my mouth to explain that no one would be seeing the remains, but I didn't have the energy, I just walked away. Later I saw him where the rest of the media had gathered; he waited like everybody else.

Suddenly my family was in front of me; Stella encouraging me with her smile, my two daughters, Bianca and Lydia, in pretty dresses and eyes full of wonder. My beautiful mother and father – how small they looked, how nervous; how brave they were to come, to walk through this sea of Indigenous eyes and into this circle. My brother too, in his fine lawyer's suit; I'd invited him but hadn't expected him to show up – he was the practical, rational son, I was the dreamer. But Mary had been a big part of his life too, and now here he was, stepping into the unknown when he was supposed to be in court. Big Rob ushered my family to their places and made sure they were comfortable. I invited some of the ladies from the Oodgeroo Unit to sit with my family but they shook their heads. 'This business is between your family and the Wamba Wamba, darling,' one of them explained. 'Our proper place is on the outside of the circle, behind the men.'

A blur. Bob nodded to me, it was time. I took my elder daughter by the hand. 'Bianca, how would you like to be a flower girl, except with feathers?'

'A *feather* girl – can I, Mummy!?'

Stella nodded her approval. 'Just do as Daddy says.'

Bianca and I made our way to Victor's office, and I asked my daughter to wait outside while I checked on Jason. The Yorta Yorta songman had transformed himself; fully painted and chanting, he transcended the ages – he *was* past, present and future. Without saying a word I draped the Aboriginal flag over the case, placed the headdress on top, and took them quietly from the room.

The ceremony had been due to start 30 minutes earlier, but no one seemed to mind; everyone waited silently. I stood in the wings, out of sight with Mary and Bianca. Craig, still on tenterhooks, rushed over.

'We can't start yet, there are some more Brisbane elders coming; we can't start without them.'

And then, as if on cue, they came; slowly, with dignity, the men in twill jackets and hats, the women in their Sunday best and smelling of lavender. Shoe leather shone and brooches sparkled. It was only then that I realised just how significant, just how important Mary's return was. People moved aside to make sure the elders had the best vantage points, the best seats. A match lit the gum leaves and herbs that had been arranged on the coolamon; smoke curled up, up past Bob's beard, up between the grey, four-storey walls that made the courtyard feel like a cool, deep gorge. Amid the crackling leaves, the smell of eucalyptus oil, the flames dancing, time dissolved – and 100 pairs of eyes became one.

'When Jason comes out, we're going to follow,' I whispered to Bianca. 'I want you to walk in front of me and to hold the feathers out in front of you, like this.'

I demonstrated and then placed the headdress in her hands. She could barely see over it and giggled as the feathers tickled her nose.

We waited.

'KAR-AAK!'

Bianca and I jumped. There was a clack-clack of clapping sticks, and then another 'KAR-AAK!'

Jason was out of sight, around a far bend in the concrete and block canyon. His black cockatoo cries cascaded down stairwells, echoed off overhead walkway escarpments, and bounced through the air-conditioning ducts.

'Don't be scared,' I whispered in Bianca's ear; but there was no need to reassure her, she was electrified.

At last the Yorta Yorta songman emerged behind us, wrapped in a possum-skin cloak, never taking more than three or four steps before unleashing another cry or incantation to his ancestors, to Mother Earth. I could see glimpses of the gathered guests, heads down or fixed on the centre of the circle, on the fire, on the curling smoke. Jason entered the courtyard, chanting, cracking those thunderclap sticks, splitting open the atmosphere with his 60 000-year-old song. Then we followed, a few paces behind.

People parted to allow us entry into the circle, a circle now made sacred by the smoke. As we entered, a barrage of flashes and the noise of variable-speed shutters reminded us of the outside world, of what century we

were in. Bianca followed Jason, and I walked behind
her. 'Hold your head up high, sweetheart,' I whispered.
If only I'd thought things through a little better; imagine
Ebony and Bianca – black and white – walking together.
And then I noticed that Bianca was wearing the bracelet
Ebony had given her, and that symbol, however private,
had a potency all its own. I placed the case that held
Mary on the small table. With the flag hanging low
over each side and obscuring the legs, the case seemed
to float amid the grey smoke and the lightning storm
of camera flashes. Jason continued to dance and sing,
working the circle, purifying the space. And then,
silence. Again I whispered in Bianca's ear, 'Hold the
headdress high, over your head so everyone can see
the beautiful feathers.' I placed my hands around her
waist and lifted her into the air. We turned to the north,
we turned to the east and my family, we turned to the
south. I lowered Bianca and together we turned to the
west, to Mary, and placed the headdress – wreath-like –
in front of the case. I walked Bianca back to her mother
before rejoining Bob and Jason in the circle.

Mother Nature had primacy now; we mortal players
merely fumbled in the gaps between the smoke's heav-
enly dance, our utterances sounded feeble compared

to the fire's holy crackle. Bob offered formal words of welcome, Jason Wamba Wamba words of gratitude and forgiveness. Words. Words carried skyward by the smoke and cinders then scattered by hot, dry wind. Tears from the women fell like plops of rain. Jason glistened under his cloak of 30 skins while I sweated rivers in my polyester shirt and white skin. I took my unfinished speech from my pocket; droplets of sweat slipped from my brow and fell with slow motion splats onto the page. Ink ran and the words dissolved into each other. I placed the pages on the fire. This was a time for simple words: Sorry, Return, Earth. I laced these three gemstones together with short strands of sentence that I will never remember. Jason stepped forward. I handed him his ancestor and for a moment Mary lay cradled in both black and white hands. Then Jason stepped back with Mary and placed the case under the loving shade of a tree. He put his didgeridoo to his lips; it was time for a new dance now, a happier song. The breeze danced too, taking the smoke in all directions, making sure that everyone felt its healing caress. It danced ghost-like over my family, over me.

Midway through his dance, Jason could stand the heat no more. He pulled the possum-skin cloak from his shoulders and threw it into the air like a giant pizza dough. It turned in the smoke and landed fur-side down, its smooth inside revealed to us for the first time. Each of its 30 panels was decorated with a story told in a constellation of symbols. I couldn't read the panels, but I understood them; they were a map of the Wamba Wamba universe. The cloak drew me in as a telescope draws in the night sky. I felt dizzy. Jason danced over to Ashley, a songman who had come to represent the local clans. He beckoned to his fully painted northern brother with the words, 'Let's jam,' and the two didgeridoos weaved together like birds wheeling on high. A crowd of Asian students, drawn by the music, had found a vantage point on an upper balcony. Security tried to hold them back, but there were too many. They held their mobile phones high, blindly snatching photos. It didn't matter. I looked to the faces around the circle; many eyes were downcast or shut, many more were wet with tears, hankies dabbed at cheeks. I needed the smoke. I moved close to the fire and closed my eyes; the smoke coiled around me, through me. I inhaled its magic deeply, right down into the insides of my toes. Wamba Wamba words caressed my ear; I felt a hand on my shoulder, my eyes opened and met Jason's. 'It's all right, brother,' he promised, 'it's all right.'

As Bob gently patted out the fire, the old people began to drift into the circle. I watched the elders as they approached my mother and father with open hearts, wrapping my parents' nervous hands in theirs.

'Thank you. Thank you,' they repeated, their words emanating from dry lips and moist eyes in equal measure. These were the people of my parents' generation, fellow countrymen and good people all, kept apart from each other by cruel circumstance. That day I witnessed a life-long racial divide transcended by tears, smiles and handshakes. My brave father and mother had faced the music, and what sweet song of forgiveness it was.

Jason, Bob and I were taken aside for interviews while a small crowd gathered to marvel at the possum-skin cloak, which still lay open on the ground. Craig and his staff ushered people into the lunchroom, where a generous feast had been laid out. The tension had largely dissipated now, but solemnity hung in the air. There was an awkwardness, as if people weren't sure what to do; celebrate or mourn. And then the most beautiful thing happened – one of the Aboriginal girls laughed. It was a short, beautiful laugh that just escaped. The room fell silent and every eye fell upon her. With her hand over her mouth she looked around sheepishly. Then slowly, her hand dropped away to reveal her smile – and what a smile it was! That laugh was like the first bird to greet the sun after a storm has passed; within moments we were all twittering and laughing too.

Jason was the centre of attention. He was the perfect pin-up boy for Aboriginal aunties and grandmothers everywhere – manly and kind, proud yet humble too. I couldn't help notice that many of the younger Indigenous girls were watching him from afar with puppy-dog eyes. Dad was disappointed that Gary hadn't been able to attend, but luckily Jason was a football nut too, and the two talked deep football in the way that only true aficionados can. In another corner of the room, my daughters were plied with cakes, pikelets and scones by a group of Aboriginal aunties.

The students from my class stood around in a bunch with their backs turned to the festive atmosphere. They looked as though they wanted to join in but just couldn't seem to move their feet; this was a feeling I'd known for over 30 years! It reminded me of old-time

Western movies where the white folk set their wagons in a circle at night to fend off Indian attack. I poked my head into the perimeter and with a gentle nudge suggested, 'If you guys want to meet some Indigenous people, now might be a good time.'

Craig wandered over with a thank-god-that's-over smile.

'Is Mary okay just sitting out there?' he asked, tilting his head in Mary's direction. Jason had left the case in the courtyard under the headdress and flag. A few people gave it a wide berth as they walked past. But just as I was about to suggest to Jason that we move Mary to somewhere more private I noticed how much warmth and goodwill was pouring out through the lunchroom doors – it was like human sunshine.

'It's his party,' I replied, 'let's leave him there to enjoy it for a few more minutes.'

There was little talk on the way back to Bob's house, we were all too emotionally drained; even Bob's imaginary brake pedal got a rest.

'Nice place you got here, brother,' said Jason as we pulled into the driveway.

'It's just a bed,' said Bob, implying that his real home was his country.

I walked Bob to his front steps and thanked him for all he'd done.

'Bob, I want to keep going,' I said, 'I want to stay with this, I want to help.' For the past two weeks I'd ridden an extraordinary wave, and now its energy was ebbing. I lay on the sand amid sea foam as the wave returned once more to the sea.

'You have helped,' Bob replied a little wearily, not just from the day's events, but in a way that suggested he'd been confronted with over-enthusiastic white converts-to-the-cause before. 'You need to understand that there's a feeling in our community that *we* need to help ourselves.'

He left me with a smile and turned away. I was feeling like that jellyfish again, high and dry.

I drove Jason to his hotel in town. I'd invited him home for dinner, but he wanted a quiet night. He asked if I knew of any good Thai restaurants. 'Brother, I am addicted to Thai food, I could eat it three times a day.'

Again I was caught off guard. I chuckled to myself;

what was I expecting the man to eat, witchetty grubs?

We pulled into the driveway of the hotel. It was a five-storey mock Georgian affair, the sort of place you'd expect to be called the Dorchester or Winchester.

'Wow, nice place!' I said, genuinely impressed.

Jason got out with his didgeridoo, dufflebag full of possum-skin magic, and Mary.

'Mate, it's *real* flash all right. When I checked in they told me there was a problem and I thought, oh no here we go.' Jason rolled his eyes for effect, suggesting he'd expected to be turned away due to a no-Afro, no-didgeridoo door policy. 'But it wasn't what I'd thought, they'd double-booked my room, and guess what, they upgraded me to a bigger suite!'

I laughed, once again marvelling at Jason's ability to draw out the best in people.

'There was one condition, though; they made me promise to put on a little concert on the didge later.'

As he walked towards the polished brass and spotless glass of the revolving door, he turned. 'John, it's as if there's been someone watching over me on this trip. Every single person I've met has been just beautiful.'

I couldn't have agreed more.

Dja Dja Wurrung and Wamba Wamba Elder, Gary Murray, dressed in the Wamba Wamba ceremonial cloak with a Dja Dja Wurrung Bark etching.

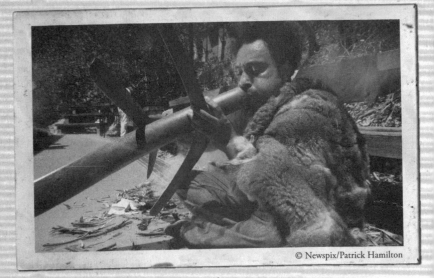

© Newspix/Patrick Hamilton

Yorta Yorta songman Jason Tamiru presides over Mary's 2005 handover ceremony.

Kamilaroi Elder and repatriation specialist Bob Weatherall.

Jason Tamiru receives the Wamba Wamba Ancestor.

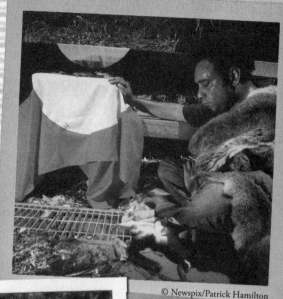

MP78073

■ Embrace . . . Jason Tamiru and John Danalis.

Remains returned

RAW emotion ran high at QUT Kelvin
Grove recently when the 200-year-old remains of an Aboriginal man were returned

Jida Murray-Gulpilil, dancer, musician and cultural man. "No one can touch him."

Aboriginal Australia.

Photo by Jida Gulpilil © John Danalis

John Danalis watches the Murray River
slide by from Wamba Wamba country.

Jida Gulpilil-Murray and Jason Tamiru preparing the reburial graves. Mary's black case sits between the two men.

"They came from all over Victoria and N.S.W." Traditional Owners and guests place gum leaves upon the Wamba Wamba Ancestral remains.

Clayton Mitchell-Murray, Adam Lampton, Jason Taniru (sitting) and Jida Gulpilil-Murray welcome and smoke guests to the sacred Menera burial grounds. Mary's resting place is in the far paddock behind Jida.

Mary's Billabong.

Mary © Wiran Aboriginal Corporation

Kumba

Nguteyuk kurruk pa yemin-yemin

Lie down and sleep
Your country and burial ground

CHAPTER
TWELVE

{ 13 OCTOBER 2005 }

I ding-dinged the little ships bell by my parents' front door and let myself in. Stepping through the doorway – a doorway I had walked in and out of all my life – I noticed a change that stopped me in my tracks. The air, the energy, *something* felt different, looser. It was like walking into an empty house after the removalists had been, but everything was just where it had always been – everything except Mary. There was a sense of lightness, of cleanliness, of wellbeing.

'We made the front page,' I said as I passed Mum

the local paper. A photograph covered almost the entire page; it was close-up of Jason and me in an emotional embrace after the handover. Two men hugging; not the sort of thing that usually makes front page news! The funny thing was I couldn't even remember the hug taking place. We'd made the television news too; my father pressed the Play button on the VCR and made us watch the story three times. It was interesting seeing the ceremony from a different perspective, seeing it condensed down to a one-minute news story, without all the behind-the-scenes uncertainty and fumbling – I was pleased.

Jason was waiting as I pulled up at the hotel.

'Man, how did you sleep last night?' he asked as we loaded his gear and Mary back into the car.

'Best sleep I've *ever* had,' I answered, 'I just fell back into this black hole and woke up feeling amazing – totally rested.'

'Me too!' he said. 'I got home from dinner and just collapsed, wow, what a sleep, I feel brand-new!'

Jason was a little worried about getting Mary onto the plane. He explained that he'd phoned the airline to make sure he'd be able to take Mary on as hand luggage.

'The airline said they'd need some sort of official papers, but when I asked them who to contact, nobody in the office could tell me.'

'Maybe this will do the trick.' I reached into the back seat and grabbed the local and state newspapers.

'Hey, front cover! Man, that's a beautiful picture, I've gotta get a copy of this to take home for Gary.'

'It's yours,' I said. 'And check out the *Courier Mail*, page 11, and a guy from the *Australian* was there too, so we'll be in that paper too. Mate, if they give us any trouble at the airport, I'll just wave these under their noses. Nobody will want to mess with Mary's return home, this is news.'

But there would be no trouble. When Jason checked in and explained what was in the camera case the attendant's eyes lit up. 'Yes, we heard you were coming. I'll just let the duty manager know you've arrived.'

The Yorta Yorta songman received the red-carpet treatment; they handled his didgeridoo as if it belonged to the Queen, and when the attendant wished Jason and Mary a safe journey home, she said it with a sincerity that encapsulated the goodwill of every well-wisher that we had encountered over the last couple of days. The manager escorted us to the security counter and then turned to us apologetically. 'I'm terribly sorry, but I'm afraid that the case will still have to go through the X-ray machine.'

'Hey, not a problem,' said Jason, placing the case on the little conveyor belt.

Word of our arrival had preceded us, for more security officers than seemed necessary had gathered behind the X-ray monitor to watch Mary pass through. I couldn't resist a last glimpse and without a word the security people made room so I could see my old friend one last time. Jason didn't seem to mind all the interest but was careful to look the other way as Mary disappeared beneath the black rubber drapes and into the bowels of the machine. Mary lay on his side surrounded by the garland of leaves from my garden; the monitor's picture was all greys and blues, and as he passed through he looked distinctly regal, like the sideways bust of a Roman emperor on an old silver coin.

'What a journey you've had,' I whispered as the case emerged out the other side. As we made our way up to the departure lounge I asked Jason if he'd opened the case. 'You know, for a peek.'

He turned to me with a horrified look. 'Of course not! That's not my business, that's for the old ones.' I still hadn't learnt to think before opening my trap.

We found the gate and sat in a quiet spot.

'I'll send the case back after the burial, is that okay?' Jason asked.

'No, keep it, as a thank-you, use it for your work. Anyway, how did you get into repatriation?'

Jason told his story, of how he'd been awarded an internship at the Melbourne Museum. He had loved the job and was proud to be a part of the museum's Indigenous unit and program.

'It was all about keeping our culture alive. Anyway, I was keen, curious – I wanted to learn, to get more knowledge so I could pass it back to our people. I used to poke around in the storerooms, but my boss used to try and distract me, to divert my attention elsewhere, and soon I found out why.'

Jason's eyes darkened. 'One day I tripped over this box, literally tripped over it. I opened it up, and inside were the remains of my people. Can you imagine that? They tried to keep it a secret from the dumb young blackfella. The more I looked, the more I found. Well, I started making noise, asking questions: "Why do you need all these old ones, what use are they, why can't they go back to country?"'

Jason sat silently.

'Well, what did they say?' I asked.

'Research, they said, we need them for research.' He spat the words out like pieces of rotten food.

'"Well, show me," I said, "show me the research." And you know what, they couldn't show me one bit, not one paper. And after all these years – decades, man! – that my people have been jammed in boxes with little metal tags attached to them as if they weren't even human beings.'

I sat there, not knowing what to say. I couldn't even imagine how it would feel to suddenly discover that your ancestors, your family, had been stashed away in boxes, drawers and bags all around your workplace – the place where you spent a sizeable proportion of your time, a place that helps define who you are.

'They wanted me to be quiet, but how could I, *how could I*, these are my people, my great-grandfather could have been in one of those boxes. In the end they said I was disruptive, I had to go, I had to leave the job I loved.'

Jason explained that that's how he got involved

with his Uncle Gary in the repatriation struggle, not just for the return of remains, but for access to and for custodianship of all their cultural heritage.

'I'm working on the other side now. These institutions have to pretend that they're working with us, you know, so they look good in public, but they don't respect us. They don't understand what these things mean to us, they don't have a clue.'

The departure lounge had begun to fill up. Business-men and women feigned interest in newspaper articles and laptop screens, but from their straining ears and furtive peeps I knew they were being drawn into Jason's story as much as I was.

'Did you know about the barks that came out from England, did Gary ever you tell you about those?'

My mind went back two weeks, to the photo I'd found on the internet of Gary wrapped in the cloak holding what looked like a shield.

'Yeah, I do remember reading about those. You took the British and Melbourne museums to court to try to keep them here, in Australia.'

'That's it.' Jason was delighted that I knew what he was talking about. 'Well, I tell you, they came out on loan from the British Museum, went on display here and it was like – whoa! – we didn't even know this kind of wood carving was part of our heritage. After they cleared all us Kooris from the land, they cut down all the big old trees, including all the ones that were carved. These barks are the only ones left in the world. None of us knew we made these things, it was lost knowledge. Well, suddenly all the young fellas are studying these barks real close, trying to read the symbols, trying to work out what kind of tools they used, and the next thing you know we're all carving barks like crazy, we had an exhibition, we were reconnecting!'

I looked at Jason and saw that the brightness had returned to his eyes. We sat quietly for a few minutes; sometimes you can say more with your mouth shut.

'Can you do me a favour?' I asked.

'You name it, brother, anything,' said Jason, looking ahead.

'Mary's packed in lemon myrtle leaves. When you, or whoever puts Mary back into the ground, can you put a branch or two into the earth with him – if that's okay?'

He gently patted the case which rested between us. 'Consider it done. Tell you what, we'll put some on the fire too, so some of that good smoke can blow up your way, eh.'

The call to board the plane came and we wandered over to the queue shuffling towards the gate.

I asked Jason if there was a girlfriend waiting for him at the other end. He shook his head.

'I tell you what, you turned a few heads yesterday. I reckon you made a few of those Murrie girls go very weak at the knees. Some of them were gorgeous too.'

'No way!' he said, 'I didn't notice any girls, I couldn't. I was responsible for the business; *everything* I had went into that.'

Again, I wished I had kept my trap shut, but Jason didn't seem annoyed. We approached the gate; he put down the case and opened his arms to embrace me. As we hugged, the Yorta Yorta songman said softly, almost as if to comfort me, 'Brother, oh my brother.'

As I watched Jason pull his boarding pass from the back pocket of his baggy jeans, I had that left-behind feeling again, the feeling that the wave was rolling on without me. And then, just as he was about to vanish into the boarding tunnel with Mary, the songman turned and called out, 'Now you and your family come down and see us *any* time, you're one of our mob now.'

That night the phone rang. It was Gary and Jason. They'd just crossed into Wamba Wamba country and had pulled over the car so they could call and tell me Mary was home; back in country. Gary painted me a sketch. The sun was fat and low, bathing the Riverine plains in pre-dusk gold. I could hear the silence that surrounded them. Then, all of a sudden a choir of frogs – 500 voices strong – started croaking and singing from a damp hollow somewhere near the car. The great noise pealed up the phone line, out of the earpiece and tumbled joyously into my office. It was impossible to talk, and anyway, who were we to interrupt this raucous hymn. Gary just laughed and laughed.

I phoned my parents with the news that Mary was safely home. My mother began to cry and in between her sobs she told my father. I heard him honk into the man-sized hanky he always carried.

'Those people today – just so beautiful and kind – not one bad word – just kindness.' Mum could barely get the words out. 'Your father can't come to the phone, he's too emotional to talk now – oh those people – just so beautiful.'

Tears bathed my cheeks and fell into the little holes of the telephone mouthpiece, disappearing like raindrops into a parched earth. Right then, during that phone call, my parents taught me a lesson; that it's never too late to learn, that it's never to late to change. The moment I put the phone down, rain fell like a curtain from the night sky. We needed it too. It hadn't rained for a long, long time.

CHAPTER
THIRTEEN

{ 14 OCTOBER 2005 }

The wave of Mary's return had washed me back onto
the shore, but the land I had returned to would never
be the same. All morning, friends and acquaintances
who had seen or heard the story in the news phoned
or emailed, sometimes with just a simple, 'Well done,'
but often they wanted – needed – to know more.
Depending on how I thought each person would react
to the more otherworldly aspects to the story, I told
either a short version or a long version. The long
version took at least fifteen minutes to recount, and if

the listener was particularly receptive, could take much longer. After each telling, whether long or short, I put down the phone, physically and emotionally drained – as if I'd been through a reliving of the last two weeks.

Shortly after lunch, one of the women from the Oodgeroo Unit phoned. She was distraught.

'Have you seen what they've done with Jason's picture?'

'Who has, what?' I asked, concerned, but equally relieved that I wasn't the cause of her distress.

She explained that one of the big media corporations had posted on their website a picture of Jason taken at the handover.

'Wait till you read the story,' she cried.

I typed in the address as she read it out and promised to phone back after I'd taken a look. Seconds later the news page materialised, with a close-up photograph of Jason playing the didgeridoo. It was a well-composed picture, and everything was there: the possum-skin cloak, the flag-covered case containing Mary, the fire with its grey-white smoke curling like a spirit ghost. Then I read the headline: *Didgeridoo named an offensive weapon.*

The article was one of those light-hearted 'Isn't the

world a zany place'-type reports. It was a British story about a young man from Sussex who had smashed a window and threatened a couple of policemen with an 'Aboriginal musical instrument'. The bobbies arrested the man and charged him with possession of an offensive weapon. When the story came into the Australian newsroom, the editor must have grabbed the first photograph of a didgeridoo player he could lay his lazy hands on, and Jason's would have been wired to the newspapers the night before. I pictured a spotty kid in a three-sizes-too-large Tottenham Hotspurs shell-suit running amok with a dodgy souvenir brought home from an Australian backpacking holiday; then I looked at the picture of Jason – a songman, a custodian of culture, a future elder. Anger surged up my spine like molten lava. 'That's *my* friend! That's *our* smoke! That's Mary! Bastards!' There they were again, pulling the rug out from under something beautiful, something empowering, something that had touched so many people.

'Utter, utter bastards, I can't believe this!' I spat over and over as I stomped around the house spraying spittles of rage in my wake. I showed the picture to Stella; she groaned in disappointment and sadness.

Jason's mobile phone was out of range; I left what must have been the world's most incoherent messages. I returned to the computer and looked for a phone number for the website's editorial department. Typically, there were plenty of numbers available for people wanting advertising rates, but there was no way in, no way to challenge or call into question the veracity or integrity of the news stories which oozed from the teats of this media bovine. After ten minutes of excavating my way through the site, I reached for the phone book and found the number for the organisation's television studio in Brisbane. I asked the receptionist to put me through to the head of the newsroom. From my kitchen window I could see Mount Coot-tha, just fifteen minutes bike ride away. Four spindly television towers rose from the ridgeline. As I listened to the on-hold music, I looked to the southernmost tower and imagined the conversation in the studio offices that stood near its base. 'Where did he say he was from?' 'He didn't.' 'How many times do I need to tell you, find out where they are from, and find out what they want; your job is to weed out the nut-jobs. Ohhhh, put him on.'

A gruff voice terminated the digitised Vivaldi.

'Newsroom.'

Usually, I handle confrontations badly. I never seem to find the correct path, I'm either mealy-mouthed or my emotions run away with me and I end up saying things I regret. But right then I rewrote the textbook on assertiveness; I wanted Mary's smoke back. After listening to my story the newsroom manager said a few choice words about his interstate colleagues and happily looked up the number for the news desk for Sydney.

I'd learnt many lessons over the last two weeks, and one lesson was this; hesitate and you'll lose your nerve.

I punched in the number. Another young, smooth-voiced receptionist answered, but before she'd finished her sentence I rolled straight over her.

'John Danalis, head of news please.'

My tone was low, forceful yet restrained; it was my impression of a media-savvy voice.

Without saying another word she put me through to a slightly older female voice.

'John Danalis, head of news, please.'

The way I said my name worked a treat, as if she – indeed everybody – should know who I was.

'Ohh, yes, one moment.'

I rolled through one office after another until I came to a stop at the desk of a senior editor; I wasn't rolling any further until I explained myself. My voice had run out of bluff and my meagre assertiveness reserves were almost depleted. I had nothing left but honesty.

'Your website is displaying an image that is causing a great deal of upset to the Indigenous communities in two separate states, to a university, and to me. It's only been up for a few hours, but if it stays up it's going to cause an almighty stink.' I explained that yesterday's ceremony was the spiritual and cultural culmination of a journey that had touched many people.

'That smoke is sacred and it has no business next to a story about some moron in Britain. You have no idea how much offence this is causing.' But from the way my voice wavered – pulled apart between anger and sorrow – I'm sure she understood.

She took down all my details and promised to get back to me within half an hour and gave me her direct number and name just to reassure me.

Ten minutes later the phone rang. This *was* the head of news and he had exactly the sort of media voice I'd been trying to affect.

'John, I wanted to let you know personally that our

people are pulling the picture as we speak, it'll be gone in a minute, so no harm done, eh.'

I blabbered a few protestations – 'You're supposed to be professionals, a first-year journalism student wouldn't make this mistake.'

'Look, the editor on this one was a Kiwi, so we can't expect too much from him, can we?' he laughed.

I couldn't believe what I was hearing. 'They're supposed to be more switched on about cultural matters than we are!'

He bounced back with a smarmy chuckle; this guy was like one of those blow-up punching clowns. 'Lo-o-ok, no harm done, eh?' His voice reached down the phone line and patted me on the shoulder.

My skin crawled. I could almost hear the rattle of his chunky gold bracelet. 'Well, there was, actually . . .' But I was out of fight; at least Mary, Jason and the smoke would soon be out of the greasy grasp of the tabloid media. 'But thanks for sorting things out.'

Five minutes later, when I hit the Refresh button on the computer, the picture was gone.

Jason phoned later in the day. 'Hey, I got your message,

something about my photo, you sounded upset.'

I explained what had happened, and that I was thinking about making a formal complaint.

'Welcome to our world,' Jason laughed.

I was silent, stunned by my friend's lack of indignation.

'Look, thanks for getting them to take it down,' he said, 'but just let it go now, save your energy for the big fights.'

'Let it go? But it was your photo they misused!'

'Hey, do you think this is a one-off?' he said, 'This happens one hundred times a day to us; ever notice that whenever they show a negative story on the news about Aboriginal people they nearly always run it with pictures of blackfellas sitting under a tree, as if that's *all* we do. And most of the time the pictures they use don't even relate to the people in the story, could be some mob from the other side of the country. I used to get angry, but if I got upset every time it happened it would kill me. It's better to laugh and stay strong.'

After the call I thought about what Jason had said. He was right, but I'd never understood enough, or cared enough to notice. I'd just spent almost three weeks getting to know quite a few Aboriginal people, and not once did I see one sitting under a tree. Not that sitting about under a tree is a bad thing; there should be more of it. In fact, take a walk through any city park at lunchtime or on the weekend and you'll see scores of Westerners, Asians, Middle Easterners, Africans, South Americans and Laplanders sitting under trees. Why doesn't the media represent those groups as 'under-tree sitters'? But how often do we see photos of Aboriginal people doing 'normal' everyday activities? Like walking the kids to school, reading a book, or enjoying a Thai curry!

CHAPTER
FOURTEEN

{ NOVEMBER – DECEMBER 2005 }

I had a lot of catching up to do. I was behind on all my assignments and exams were fast approaching, but somehow I muddled though. Occasionally I would wander through the courtyard where Mary's handover had taken place. With every visit the ceremonial ashes and burnt stick ends became harder and harder to find. After a few weeks there was no trace left. At the end of semester, when most of the students raced back to their lives, part-time jobs and holidays, I stayed on. The library had an extensive Indigenous Studies collection:

textbooks, art books, essays, maps, literature, films and music. As I waded into this secluded cultural waterhole, the bottom fell away beneath my feet into a sheer 60 000-year-old drop.

I returned to the shore each night with new material drawn from the shelves at random. By day I read and by night I watched movies and documentaries. The weathered face of actor and dancer David Gulpilil, as timeless and familiar as Uluru, became a regular presence on our television screen. Didgeridoo and clapstick song filled our lounge room and drifted like smoke through the wooden louvres and out into our street. I marvelled at the effect these rhythms, chants and beats had on Bianca and Lydia; they would move about unconsciously with fingers splayed, as if they'd already been taught these brolga dance steps. They *knew* how to move to this music, it was as if the rhythms simply reached in and awoke something that was lying dormant, the way a bee pollinates a flower.

Initially it was hard to come to grips with Aboriginal culture and society; its mind-bending timeline; its astonishingly distinct yet interwoven diversities. In many ways it reminded me of the complexity of Europe. Imagine doing a crash course on European peoples, their cultures, languages, cuisine, art, architecture, folktales, myths and belief systems, and then trying to summarise in a few neat paragraphs what it means to be European; it would be an impossible task. And yet that is largely the shallow representation of Aboriginal Australia that was presented to me when I was a young person – a mere caricature, the man on the two-dollar coin.

There is no single entry point into Aboriginal Australia, no passport office; there are – or were – over 250 language groups, for a start. For me, learning about the traditional owners of this land is like studying a beautiful but maddening jigsaw puzzle in which each piece can often be a jigsaw in itself. In fact this jigsaw is not flat, it's like a multi-dimensional matrix that co-exists in this moment, in the past 60 000 years, and in the future. Within this jigsaw lives a spiritual philosophy that enables Aboriginal people – at least those 'in culture' – to co-inhabit the rational and spiritual realms simultaneously. And similarly, there is embedded a practical resilience that has allowed Indigenous society to absorb and embrace elements of the industrialised world while keeping its cultural centre largely intact.

Emotionally, too, this puzzle both confounds and surprises Western understanding; a piece may be heavy with despair, but turn it over and there is enough laughter and joy to lift the sky. Some of the pieces are off-limits to outsiders, while great chunks of the puzzle have – particularly in the last 200 years – been obliterated forever. It is a living, evolving jigsaw, with new and exciting pieces being continually re-discovered, re-interpreted, and created afresh. The Aboriginal cultural heritage is a treasure cave, and once you walk inside and awaken to its crystalline insights, truths and tenets, it is impossible to look at the world in the same way again. Perhaps this is why white Australia has forever been perplexed by Aboriginal peoples, because despite our industry, despite our busyness, we've always suspected that these people were onto something, that they had mastered the art of living.

On the afternoon after Mary's handover, when Bob told me his people preferred to 'do it on their own', I'd felt abandoned. I had walked with the Wamba Wamba for almost three weeks, and now it was as if I'd woken up in a forest camp to find only the smouldering remains of a fire and everyone gone. On the library shelves and within the pages of books, I searched for footsteps. There were so many trails to follow. Some led to places of abundant beauty where man and Nature were perfectly aligned; others led to places in the landscape cleft open by brutality, places where the stink of death still lingers.

I pieced together information on the Wamba Wamba from slender textbook chapters, pioneer reflections, old press clippings, and oral histories. I took a 20-year-old Wamba Wamba dictionary – an all-too-rare example of a recorded Indigenous language – from the shelves with trembling hands. It was the only Aboriginal-language dictionary in the library collection and appeared never to have been borrowed or read – a mother tongue so far from country. I leafed through it to the one word I knew, Wiran – black cockatoo. The dictionary joined the growing pile of Indigenous books by my bedside table. Slowly, slowly, I began to catch glimpses of Mary.

I had seen Mary once before. I was no more than four or five, and had never been told what I could and could not see. I was in the lounge room alone, driving a Matchbox car through the carpet, lost in that lazy space between two thoughts. I looked up across the room and there before the window, backlit by the morning light, stood a dark, naked figure. He was short and slender; a teenager or in his early twenties. We stared at one another, both of us equally surprised, almost embarrassed to have intruded into each other's world. And then he simply took a sideways step behind the floor-length curtains and was gone. After a little while I walked across the room and peeked behind the curtains, but he was no longer there. I looked back across the room to where I had been playing and there on the shelves, looking back at me, sat Mary. The more I tried to remember what the person looked like, the more he faded from my memory; as if the effort of remembering was erasing the very thing it was struggling to hold onto, until eventually he was reduced to a silhouette. In the years that followed, every so often I'd try to catch out my phantom friend. I'd be playing or watching television when I would sense that I was being watched; suddenly I'd spin my head in the direction in which he had first appeared. But he was too clever now, he would forever be one step ahead, until eventually I rarely thought of him. And now, over 30 years later, as I pieced together fragments of understanding, Mary re-formed in my minds eye, not just as a naked silhouette but as a Wamba Wamba man wrapped in culture, wrapped in a possum-skin cloak. And when I closed my Western empirical eyes and looked through the eye of dreaming, this is what I was shown.

At first I glimpsed Mary only from a distance, walking through the trees on the far side of the riverbank, separated by grainy mists and the inexorable flow of time. As my knowledge grew, I crossed the river and began to wander into his camp in the pre-dawn twilight, past the sleeping dogs, like a ghost from the future. I would see his face and he would awaken with eyes startled wide. Suddenly, as if to disrupt the intrusion, an unseen hand would heft a log to the slumbering fire and Mary's face would disappear into a shower of embers and grey smoke. And then, when the smoke cleared, the clan, their cloak-lined humpies, their braces of spears, their coolamons – everything was gone.

With each visit I began to learn new things about Mary. When he looked at Nature he saw himself, not as separate, nor superior. He was Nature and she expressed herself through him. I saw him as a baby, lovingly bundled up within the voluptuous folds of his mother's 31-pelt cloak. On early winter mornings his head would venture out until the chill bit his plump cheeks, forcing him to rebury himself until the sun had sufficiently chased away the frost. His nose soon learnt to recognise the aroma of baked Murray cod and roasted yams, which would draw him out from his furry cocoon into the world and into the life around the campfires. As he grew, he watched the ceremonies and dances from inside his mother's cloak. For certain dances and songs he would be placed on his father's cloak as the women of the clan fashioned their cloaks into thundering drums by stretching them tightly over crossed legs.

I watched from afar, hidden in long grass, as the cloak became a sling that carried Mary royally around while his mother and aunties went about their business of collecting food and resources from the river, forests, plains and marshes. I listened in on their stories, gossip and laughter; not understanding the Wamba language, but still *understanding*. I saw Mary's favourite uncle too, who would pretend to sneak up on him and attempt to squeeze his cheek before he could burrow back giggling to the safety of his possum-skin lair.

As Mary grew older, the winters became cramped

under his mother's cloak. I heard his mother harangue Mary's father and his 'no-good-lazy' uncles that the child needed a cloak of his own and that it was time to gather possum skins. There exists a drawing and notes made by an early European traveller that beautifully describes the process of cloak-making. In the background of the picture, a group of hunters are smoking possums from two trees. Fires are lit in the hollowed-out trunks, while other hunters have scaled the trees and wait between the possum nests and the safety of the higher branches. Once the frightened possums emerge from their dark nooks and sleepy crannies, they are chased earthwards to the waiting clubs of the hunters below.

The possums were then skinned and the meat placed on the cooking fires while the pelts were cleaned of all fat and sinew with shell and stone scrapers. We know from the early drawings and notes of explorers that possum skins were pegged to sheets of bark and dried out by the fire or simply left in the sun and periodically rubbed with goanna oil and ash. Once the skins were dry they were pulled backwards and forwards – massaged – over the smooth, thick roots of river gums to soften the skin. Then they were ready to be stitched together with long, thin strips of animal sinew.

As Mary grew, so too did his cloak, with new pieces added as he progressed towards manhood. The soft inner pelts were inscribed with symbols, stories, and representations of significant places in Wamba Wamba landscape. With each oyster-shell incision, knowledge and Law was preserved and passed on. The coat required periodic maintenance also, and each time Mary applied oils and fat to weather-proof his dream-coat, like a blind reader of braille, his fingers retraced and refreshed themselves on the knowledge and wisdom within its scarified lining.

Mary was never the same age twice during my visits, for in the timeless time there is no chronology. At times he was a proud young father, at others he suckled upon his mother's breast. But I never saw him beyond the age of 30. On my last visit I saw his clan walk silently from a large camp oven, their backs and shoulders low with sorrow as they disappeared into the forest. I saw the freshly dug earth and knew my friend sat beneath in the traditional burial crouch, arms bound around his pulled-up legs, wrapped in his possum-skin cloak.

These are not the fantasies or delusions of a white fellow from the suburbs. I crept into the camps; I felt the dull crunch as dew-damp forest litter yielded to the weight of my twenty-first-century boots. I saw a soft-bearded Mary and the slumbering backs of his family as surely as I see my own when I walk through my house at night. And I saw more besides, but there is no need to give away everything, because in a strange way that would make me a thief. Perhaps I should have turned back then; slipped quietly from the camp, back across the river and into the safety of my own world. If I'd done so, then this story would be at its end. But instead I kept following.

CHAPTER FIFTEEN

{ DECEMBER 2005 – JUNE 2006 }

I tracked the Wamba Wamba from two centuries in the future, but I was always behind, we always will be, so much has been obliterated. Like the once-abundant bush tucker that was ripped from the earth by the jaws of sheep that swept north like a foaming king tide. Like the millions of Riverine gum trees that were felled for railway sleepers, or simply ringbarked and left to wither because they were in the way. Like the Murray River herself, blinkered by levees, siphoned and pumped of her wild and bountiful spirit. But sometimes it is possible to catch glimpses of the former landscape, for despite her ravaged surface Mother Earth still hums her gentle cantatas on morning mists, amid the snags and eddies of the river, and within patches of forgotten forest – the longer you sit, the more you see. And so I began to see more, not just of Mary and the Wamba Wamba, but of the other Riverine clans, and clans from far beyond the river too.

In my mind's eye, I marvelled at the boating skills of grey-bearded old men as they poled the simplest of bark watercraft through an ever-changing water-world dictated by the Murray's pulsating moods. I watched with envy the excited processions as whole clans trekked to the lakeside, and highland gatherings that served as festivals, tournaments, marketplaces and feasts. I wandered far from the Riverine plains into large-scale, permanent stone settlements that our history books claimed did not exist. I was astonished by highly developed systems of trading that traversed the entire continent.

I crept to the margins of ceremonies, eavesdropped at initiations that took Aboriginal men from boyhood to manhood, manhood to elder, and felt the paucity of my own culture so bereft of rites. My soul grew in understanding as I learnt about the Law as gifted to the earth by the supreme creator Biame. I looked around me and for the first time saw the earth, water and sky as a living, vibrating cathedral spinning in celestial perfection.

My father, in his own way, had embarked on his own odyssey, and although his approach was far more relaxed than mine, it was no less profound considering his conditioning. Two days after the handover my parents phoned again; they *needed* to talk about the experience.

'You know, son,' said my father, his voice breaking with emotion, 'I've had to rethink sixty years of attitude. Those people, every one of them was such a pleasure to talk to. They were all just so *friendly*, so *well presented*, so *clean*.' I almost choked as he said the word 'clean'. I was about to say something, but smiled instead at the realisation of how far my father had journeyed in the last two days; all from just one interaction, one *real* contact which had lasted less than three hours.

A week later Dad phoned again. He'd had an idea and he was excited.

'Listen, son, I've been thinking, you know that big old grindstone in the back yard?' He was referring to the wheelbarrow-sized grindstone that he'd dragged from a dry Central Queensland creekbed over 30 years ago. The stone was crisscrossed in deep grooves formed by decades, perhaps centuries, of axe-head and spear sharpening. This stone exudes a steady radiance, as if it has somehow stored within its molecules the ambient energy of all those toolmakers who sat before it. As a child I regularly ran my hands along its deep, cool grooves and channels, my five little fingers like antennae, reconnecting with the patient labours of long ago. And now Dad was proposing that Aboriginal students share the same experience.

'When your mother and I took that trip to London,' he said, referring to a holiday they'd taken in the early 1990s, 'I'll never forget how the stonework there affected me. Seeing all those worn-away steps, entranceways and cobbles – already worn away before the First Fleet even sailed! It made me think about all the people who came before us and will continue to follow; it gave me some sort of perspective, I suppose.'

'That's exactly how I felt when I was there,' I said, recalling the worn stonework of England, eroded water-like by time's passing footsteps.

'Well, I reckon that grindstone would have the same

effect on Aboriginal people, especially the young city ones who haven't spent much time in the bush. After the ceremony I thought about the courtyard, what a peaceful place it was – imagine if that grindstone was set up there with a bit of a plaque, people could go and run their hands over it for years to come, long after we're gone.'

I agreed with my father, and in my imagination I *could* see Aboriginal students reconnecting and drawing strength up through their hands; retracing the grooves and furrows of the past and with every infinitesimal finger-stroke adding their own story to this rock of ages. But not just Indigenous fingertips; the open hands of all races could acknowledge the past and add to the songlines within the stone.

'Listen, son, can you let the University know that I'd like to donate the grindstone? Tell them I've got a one-tonne ute, but they'll need to round up a few strong blokes to lift it, it's bloody heavy; we had to use a tractor to pull it from the creekbed.'

As far as Dad was concerned it was all sorted – one quick phone call and the grindstone would sit in its new home happily ever after. I was moved by my father's new-found goodwill and zeal, but at the same time alarm bells were pinging in my ears. Where had the stone come from; who were the rightful owners? Was it a sacred stone to be accessed by males only?

I cleared my throat. 'Listen, Dad, I love that stone too and I know how much it would mean to you to give it back, but there are all sorts of politics and protocols involved, we'll have to approach the rightful owners first—'

Dad made one of his bristling grunt sounds, the kind that roughly translated into 'What a lot of bullshit!'

'Look, besides all that, I think we'd better cool it for a while, everyone's just getting over the last handover. Let's give it few months. If I ring up now they'll start thinking the Danalis family are a mob of bloody pirates; they'll be wondering what else you've got stashed away under the house!'

Dad burst out laughing. 'You're probably right, son, let's give it a few months. You'll know when the time is right.'

But my father's change of heart didn't end there. A few months later he phoned and asked me if I wanted to go to the movies. Dad is a devotee of the action thriller genre; if it involves galloping horses, nuclear submarines or bent CIA agents, he's in celluloid heaven. So it came as shock when he invited me to see *Ten Canoes*, an Aboriginal-language film with all-Aboriginal cast set in Arnhem Land. I'm not sure if I spent more time during those 92 minutes watching Dad or the movie. He sat between my mother and me happily chomping popcorn; gone was the tension I'd sometimes witnessed as a boy when Aboriginal faces – particularly those of activists or demonstrators – would appear on the television screen before him. He was relaxed, comfortable.

I should have followed my father's example, happily reconciling past and present and just gotten on with life. But I couldn't stop there, I had to keep scratching, I had to dig deeper. I followed the Wamba Wamba closer to the coming of my own people, closer to my own time, and as I did so my mind began to fall apart.

There had been visitors to Victoria's shores before – unrecorded seafarers, documented explorers, whalers and sealers – but the effects of the new settlement at Port Phillip reverberated across the Aboriginal world like a cannonball being dropped into a glassy-surfaced billabong. Many clans rode the initial waves, often adapting to and accommodating the visitors as gracious yet curious hosts. But the waves from colonisation and settlement were unrelenting, pushing ever outward. The combined force of the waves equated to a tsunami, and here there were no Blue Mountains to slow its surge, to allow the Indigenous peoples to catch their breath. The clans of south-eastern Australia had unwittingly prepared the land for a rapid European pastoral expansion through centuries of burning and land management. Within a few short years of Victorian settlement in this arcadia, the old men I had 'witnessed' in their slender craft were swamped. The parties of family groups making their way to the annual Bogong moth feasts and the annual fishing festival on Lake Albert were swept away. The fires and smoke which presided over eons of ceremonies and knowledge were doused and all but extinguished.

My days became increasingly boxed in by the saddest of books, whose pages carried the anguished cry of a culture dumped on its head. I read accounts of possum-skin cloaks traded for flimsy, perpetually damp blankets, of daughters and wives being traded for rum and tobacco, of a society whose legs were kicked from beneath it by misguided good intention, neglect, treachery and brutality. And it was the brutality that brought me to *my* knees. Like many Australians, I possessed a vague awareness of the frontier violence that had unrolled across the continent for well over a century after contact. But it was only a few strands of understanding; a whisper carried on the wind that unspeakable things had occurred *out there*, somewhere to the west, somewhere over the horizon. For 200 years we've made too much noise with our busyness for our collective conscience to hear. We've all sped past forlorn-looking highway signposts bearing place names like Murdering Creek, Slaughterhouse Gully and Butchers Ridge, but the meanings of these placenames barely register as we hurtle towards tomorrow at 120 kilometres an hour. And when we are occasionally confronted with the past we brush it off, believing that the violence was sporadic, short-lived and sadly inevitable. But too often, it was anything but that.

I read book after bloody book. I read of officially sanctioned vigilante parties whose members' rifle butts were proudly notched with kills from campaigns of blind and prolonged retribution. I read of craven individuals like the shepherd who tricked visiting natives into eating plaster of Paris instead of flour, and the squatter who enjoyed giving shaving demonstrations to local tribesmen using the upturned skull of one of their clan as a shaving bowl. For a while I rationalised that these were brutal times and that acts of savagery were perpetrated by both black and white. But as I waded deeper into the pages detailing the rapes, poisonings, shootings, bludgeonings and full-scale massacres, it became painfully obvious that the undeclared frontier war was a one-sided affair. And unlike traditional wars with rules of engagement and codes of conduct, here the Europeans often acted with very little honour or restraint – in fact, many of the 'engagements' were little more than human culls.

I began to wonder if I was the only whitefella in my neat little suburb who was privy to our nation's dirty secret. I bailed up friends and neighbours. Of course most people knew *something* – and lots of people knew far more than I did – only they didn't relish me standing centimetres from their faces asking, 'Do you know what we've done, do you know what we've done?' like the Colonel Kurtz character from *Apocalypse Now*. I quickly discovered that the fastest way to upset a barbecue or dinner-party host was to inform his guests that the foundations of our prosperous country are soaked through with the blood of its original owners.

The last book I read on the subject is one I would not quite finish. Bruce Elder's *Blood on the Wattle* chronicles the known history of Aboriginal murders, massacres and mistreatment so vividly, so relentlessly, that the book has earned a reputation for thrusting its readers into the depths of despair. And I was no exception! As I lay in the bath one evening, working through page after harrowing page, I came to a graphic passage in which a whooping colonial vigilante on horseback swings an hysterical Aboriginal toddler about by the legs like a polo mattock before finally dashing his head on a gum tree as he gallops by. I lay in the bath, listening to my own children playing only metres away, and in my imagination they became that little boy. As I listened to their soft voices, my fingers seemed to reach out and touch the smooth, dimpled trunk of the spotted gum in all its hardness. My wife, humming to herself in the kitchen, became the child's screaming mother, dragged by the hair by another grinning, wild-eyed horseman, her legs and buttocks smashed and torn across rocks and brush, her mind snapped by the sight of her child's crimson life-force exploding across the hardwood and into the bluest of southern skies. And as the horseman rode away to finish his work, to silence the screaming, I noticed a glinting arc of steel in his hand, and I imagined – almost believed for a moment – that it was the rusty trooper's sabre hanging on my friend Pete's wall.

I lay in the bath, unable to move. The water seemed to have turned red, mirroring the colours of waterholes into which entire communities were driven and cut down by gunfire amid the reeds. Stella came to the door, annoyed that I hadn't answered her repeated calls that dinner was about to be dished up. She looked down at me and in her face I saw my own terror reflected. She snatched the hardbound book from my hands and in a tone that both pleaded and demanded, said, 'Enough!'

I managed to conceal the true depth of my despair until a few days into the New Year. Each morning I awoke feeling as though I had been buried up to my neck in wet sand on a deserted grey beach. The Wamba Wamba were long gone. Just behind the desolate sand dunes the world rolled on like a funfair in all its boisterous beauty, and no matter how much I opened my senses to feel it, it remained untouchable. As the days progressed a smothering tide crawled towards me, around me, over me. I mouthed silent bubbles at a dazzling sky bouncing through the swirling lens of seawater. I looked down and saw my own drowning.

Suicidal feelings wormed their way into my otherwise blessed life. I had a loving wife and two button-cute little girls with endless reserves of love – yet every time I passed through my garage a coil of rope called to me. A couple of times I even walked over to it, stroked the coarse synthetic fibres and imagined its unyielding bite around the soft flesh of my neck. Mercifully, I always found enough strength to put it away, out of sight. But I knew where it was, patiently waiting until the day came when my legs would surely conspire against my soul and carry me down to its hiding place, out into the back yard beneath the sturdy bough of our jacaranda tree.

'Stella, I'm in trouble, I don't trust my legs any more, I think they are going to kill me,' I cried, breaking down one morning after the children had been packed off for the day. I told my shocked partner of 20 years about the torrent of suicidal feelings that had all but swept me away from my lifelines of love and rational thought. 'I need help, today!'

Somehow just talking about it eased the pressure enough for us to formulate a plan. We were financially stretched but I knew that the University had a free student health service which offered counselling. Minutes later I had a priority appointment.

The student services counsellor might as well have been an angel of deliverance. After the first visit I felt as though I could breathe again and by the second the awful death-tide had receded. Nevertheless, it was still out there, ready to rush in again should my mental weather darken. I was referred to a psychiatrist, who after a 40-minute consultation wisely pronounced that I was a 'rapid-cycle bipolar' but that with proper medication all would be well. I grasped at his diagnosis, relieved that my mental desperation had a name and was curable.

'I'll do whatever you recommend,' I agreed, almost kissing his Italian leather sneakers in gratitude.

For the next six months I visited the psychiatrist's reclining chair once a fortnight.

Since my first visits to the University counsellor, which involved just talking and gaining an understanding of depression, I'd certainly begun to feel better; but the drugs my new doctor prescribed were an entirely new version of hell. I'd managed to avoid the rope and its sudden final jerk, but the little pills I agreed to swallow each morning and night drained my life away in a different manner. Within weeks I was a pale, drooling shell of my former self. Friends were shocked at my appearance and phoned Stella to express their concern. My hands began to shake, making it difficult to do up even a shirt button. I found it difficult to balance on my bicycle, let alone find the energy to pump up the tyres. Whereas once I could write hundreds of words a day, now I was barely capable of finishing a sentence. My marks at university began to slide and I requested extension after extension on assignments. I slept for hours each day. In desperation Stella phoned the psychiatrist and pleaded with him, 'Yes, John was depressed, but he was never this bad, he was never like this!' The psychiatrist was incensed that my wife – a woman who has known me for over half my life – should question his judgement.

'Your husband's problem is that he is fighting the medication, he won't surrender to it, he won't comply!' he screamed down the phone. 'If I had my way I'd admit him to our private hospital for a month, that way we'd get him sorted out once and for all!' Stella was dumbfounded. 'I think he's the crazy one,' she sobbed into my shoulder.

After a few more weeks the doctor grudgingly conceded that the medication was having adverse effects and instead prescribed lithium, a once-common treatment for schizophrenia. Lithium, a toxic chemical used in batteries, is a high-risk medication that requires weekly tests to monitor its levels in the bloodstream. Now I had two heavy mood-altering drugs coursing through my body. As the blood was drained from my arm each week, the bills from my psychiatrist and weekly pathologist tests steadily drained our bank account. One day I noticed that I was no longer walking but shuffling, like the character Randall Patrick McMurphy in *One Flew Over the Cuckoo's Nest – after* the operation. And it was then I realised that the same fate was befalling me, except mine was a chemical lobotomy. Despite every last hair on my body being sedated, despite wanting to fall into a thousand-year nap, something inside me began to fight back. I realised that there was nothing inherently wrong with my mind; I was merely an artist who had bombarded his sensitive spirit with the ugly truth. I seized hold of that belief; it became my mantra, my lifeline. And as I pulled that belief closer, hand over shaking hand, I came to understand the power of the artist's way of seeing, of feeling.

I sat in the psychiatrist's waiting room leafing through the pages of his Saab Owners Club and *Epicurean* magazines and realised that this man was merely a foot soldier for the transnational drug corporations. His methodology had little to do with individual wellbeing, growth or joy – it was all about *compliance*; shuffling happily into line in this 'brave new world'. I began to run Google searches on the medications I was swallowing, and while the treatments are undoubtedly beneficial to some people, a paper mountain of dissenting opinion and contrary evidence began to accumulate in my printer tray. Drugs like the ones I was being told I would be dependent upon for a lifetime were an extraordinarily lazy and mind-bogglingly profitable solution to some of the fundamental problems which challenge the human condition.

As I commenced my four-week teacher training practice this realisation became blindingly obvious. I was placed in a local state school which had a higher-than-average proportion of children with behavioural problems: Asperger's syndrome, autism, attention-deficit disorders. I spent many hours in my first two weeks coaxing students out of trees and back into the classroom, or if need be into the special 'quiet room'. I read with interest the medical noticeboards in the staffroom outlining the various behavioural quirks, allergies, drug schedules and 'what to do in an emergency' details of each student. I observed the chemically laden, over-refined packaged foods the students pulled from their lunchboxes and bought at the tuckshop. I watched as harried parents disgorged their already stressed offspring at the school gate from hulking SUVs and thought to myself, 'Is it any wonder?'

One afternoon as I wobbled home on my bike, I emerged from a quiet, creek-side bike track near the confluence of three major roads. The contrast between the tranquillity of the remnant bush and the rivers of peak-hour cars was astonishing. I sat on a low fence and watched ten thousand defeated faces slip by; expressionless, boxed in behind tinted glass. Overhead a billboard promised happiness in a wineglass, another mateship in a beer bottle. Further along, another promised longer and more satisfying sex. On the rear of a truck I saw a bumper sticker I'd seen hundreds of times before, but for the first time understood its threatening undertone: 'AUSTRALIA. IF YOU DON'T LIKE IT, LEAVE!' I wondered, is this how Mary felt when he peered from the Barmah Forest into the margins of the new world? As I looked out at all that metal and rubber ceaselessly rushing by, everything seemed at odds with what it means to be human. And I wondered, is this what my madness means – to be able to see through the illusion, to feel things as they really are?

The next day I wandered down the hallway which led to my classroom. A young teacher was pinning up paintings along pieces of cord in front of the louvred windows. She explained that they were portraits of famous Australia explorers – Blaxland, Cunningham, Stuart, Leichhardt, all the usual suspects. Many of the artworks had a Picasso-esque quality about them and I told her I liked them very much.

'Yes, we studied Picasso in our art unit as part of our study into portraiture,' she said proudly, 'so I took the opportunity to blend elements from the art unit with our Australian history unit.'

We talked a little more about art before I added, 'Did you know that many of these explorers had Aboriginal guides and did little more than follow the walking trails and trading routes that existed for centuries? So in some ways these men didn't actually discover anything at all.' My voice swelled with an enthusiasm that I had barely known in months. 'I could bring you in some material, and by the way, have the children seen the Horton's tribal map of Australia yet? It *is* astonishingly beautiful and will change the way they think about their country forever. I really think it should be displayed prominently in every school in Australia.'

She looked at me a little strangely; perhaps she was alarmed by the excited spittle that flew off my words.

'Well, we aren't covering any Indigenous units this year, so that wouldn't really be appropriate.'

And with that she went back to pinning up a cubist Burke and Wills.

In a strange way the paintings became a turning point for me. Each time I passed those 30 bizarre portraits, a breeze would gently billow them out into the hallway as if they were breathing. It was truly unsettling, and more than once I had to close my eyes to regain my composure. It also hammered home the limitations of the current education system; these children were being taught many of the same tired old lessons I had been taught over 30 years ago. I resolved then and there never to teach from a curriculum; if I was to work with children I would teach from the heart. A week later I formally withdrew from prac and at the end of that semester from the teaching degree altogether. Resolving to free myself of the terrible chemicals that were poisoning my spirit, I found a sympathetic doctor who helped me formulate an escape plan and would monitor my withdrawal. But to get well again – to be truly healed – I knew I would have to visit Mary.

CHAPTER SIXTEEN

{ MELBOURNE, 16 APRIL 2006 }

I floated over the Victorian border at 15 000 feet in the late afternoon with my nose pressed to the little window and there it was, the Murray River shimmering below. It looked just as it is described in the creation story; those big bends carved into the land by the giant Murray cod Kurrumeruk's thrashing tail as rainbow serpent Yemurraki pursued him from the mountains, across the horizon to the sea. From this height the river looked as if it had been created yesterday; each bend caught mercurial flashes of late-afternoon sun and belted them heavenwards again, reminding me of one of the river's Aboriginal names, Millewa (stars on the water).

The land rolled away in a tapestry of patchwork properties stitched together with barbed-wire fences and bitumen. Occasionally a tiny tuft of remnant forest broke the monotony, but these lonely pieces were few and far between. No wonder the original owners were squeezed out so rapidly, so effectively. I scanned the river, hoping to recognise the settlement of Swan Hill – for only a few kilometres upstream, on the northern bank, Mary lay in Wamba Wamba soil.

I'd arranged to stay with friends in Melbourne. Craig picked me up from the airport. We hadn't seen each other for over a year, but our conversation came easily in the way it does between good friends. I didn't tell him how ill I'd been or that I'd been living in a drug-induced nightmare. Somehow just seeing the river, being closer to Mary made me feel steadier. When my friends showed me to their spare room, I stopped in the doorway. Over my bed hung a poster; a reproduction of Craig Ruddy's Archibald Prize-winning portrait of David Gulpilil. The painting, entitled *Two Worlds*, is an extraordinary work that crackles with an otherworldly intensity and energy. I lay on my bed and smiled as this colossus of Australian cinema and Indigenous culture stared across the room. I *was* getting closer.

{ 17 APRIL 2006 }

The next morning I phoned Gary. He knew I was coming and had promised to take me to the property, but he seemed far from happy to hear from me. He said something quickly about being in negotiations with the Victorian state government to save the 'sacred flame'. Gary suggested I call again later in the day, and hung up. No 'Welcome to Koori Country', not even a hello; what a disappointment! I suppose I was expecting to be greeted with wide open arms. I sat on the end of the bed for a while, staring up at David Gulpilil. In that portrait the lines in his face are rendered like stringybark; his dark eyes look towards a horizon. He seems to be waiting for something he *knows* is coming, but in his eyes there is anxiety, as if he is worried that he won't quite live to see its arrival. Perhaps I was reading things into those eyes, but they helped put things into perspective. My story was but a footnote in an epic saga. Mary's remains were but one amid tens of thousands still waiting to be returned.

And my troubled spirit was infinitesimal compared to the real struggle that affects Indigenous Australians day after day after day. Mary might have been laid to rest but the reconciling of unfinished business continues.

My hosts had left a newspaper on the breakfast table for me and as I chewed my breakfast I scanned its pages with half interest. A headline containing the words 'sacred flame' leapt out at me. No wonder Gary sounded so preoccupied. The 'sacred flame' was a ceremonial fire which burned on Melbourne's Domain, a hilltop corner in parklands only a short distance from the war memorial, the Shrine of Remembrance. The fire had been lit as an 'alternative remembrance' of Indigenous peoples and a protest camp had grown around it to shelter the keepers of the fire, and to provide comfort to those who visited it each day. Gary was fighting to overturn a court eviction notice ordering that Camp Sovereignty be dismantled.

It was a two-hour walk from my friend's house in the north of Melbourne to the Domain parklands just south of the Yarra River. As my legs carried me towards the fire, it was impossible not to be impressed by the results of 150 years of European endeavour. Melbourne is such an elegant and visually generous city; you can feel the love that has gone into her stonework, latticing and landscaping. Caught up in the bustling beauty of the city, with its tree-lined streets and fine architecture paid for with golden nuggets, it is easy to forget its original occupants.

Crossing the Yarra, I entered the parklands, searching the treeline for tell-tale smoke. Remembering the wonderfully scented lemon myrtle from my own back yard, I looked about for a fallen branch; something I could place on the fire as an offering. But as I scanned the manicured gardens, I realised that none of the trees about me were native; they all appeared to be introduced species: elms, oaks and willows. In fact the entire design of the parklands reminded me of the great public parks of London; it looked nothing like Australia. And then it dawned on me: who was I to lay a branch on the sacred fire anyway!

My nostrils found the 'sacred flame' for me. Unlike the odourless, gas-lit flame at the official Shrine of Remembrance, this flame was fed on native logs and branches which were hauled in especially. White smoke wafted about the camp, its native scents at odds with the deep green weeping foliage of the surrounding trees and the glinting office-tower backdrop of the central business district. A couple of red, black and yellow banners roughly marked out the perimeter of the camp. In my readings I'd learnt that it was traditional etiquette never to walk into a camp uninvited; one had to sit at its margins in full view of the clan, sometimes for days, before the elders felt the visitor was trustworthy and free from bad spirits. At Camp Sovereignty, a hand-painted sign politely asked visitors to do the same. I waited, a little nervously. Before all this business with Mary, I would never have dreamt of wandering into any sort of protest site, let alone an Indigenous one. Before long, two young white women joined me; they were office workers and had popped over in their lunchbreak to learn more about the fire. Soon others came: another young woman from the local art college and an impeccably dressed antique dealer in his fifties. After about ten minutes, two Koori women approached us with wide smiles. They led us into the camp, explaining that visitors were not permitted to go near the fire unless escorted. The sacred fire was set within another clearing, the perimeter of which was marked out with foot-long upright logs. 'There'll be a smoking ceremony a bit later, so we'll all get the chance to breathe in that good healing smoke,' one of the women explained. 'Come and get yourselves a hot cuppa, there's plenty of bikkies too.' A couple of folding tables were set up with provisions and a gas camp stove brought a billycan of water to the boil.

There were about a dozen Kooris at the camp and everyone made us welcome except one man whose face seemed perpetually contorted by anger.

'Why do these white bastards keep showing up,' he ranted to no one in particular, 'this fire is none of their fucking business!'

'Oh don't mind him,' said one of the other women. 'He's been here since the fire was started and he hasn't had much sleep for the last month. It's hard work watching the fire all through the night, especially in the rain. It gets windy up here too.'

The women explained that the hill we stood upon was a traditional meeting place called Mumajah, a neutral space where clans had come together for centuries.

'Big corroborees were held right here,' she said, as a breeze slowly billowed the Aboriginal flags on their makeshift bamboo poles. 'Business was conducted here too, disputes between different mobs worked out; still is. Every few days the lawyers come, the Lord Mayor has visited too. And just over there,' she said, motioning with an outstretched hand but with eyes averted from the place she was pointing to, 'lie thirty-eight of our people, returned after a long battle with the Museum. There's also generations of ancestors buried all around us.'

A little later a bearded Koori approached us. He appeared to be in his fifties or sixties – but as with Auntie Alyson, it was impossible to tell. He wore loose clothing of earthy weaves; beads, stones and feathers hung from him with transcendental potency. A green, yellow and red cap – the Rastafarian tricolour – topped off his ensemble. He smelt of the smoke; he was the smoke. I had met my first Wirinun – an Aboriginal shaman.

The Wirinun formed us, black and white, into a line and brushed us over one by one with the smoking branch of a green eucalypt sapling. Despite the smoke, the leaves felt cool, their oily freshness resisting total ignition. He explained the importance of fire and how it lay at the root of Aboriginal Law and culture. 'Fire is our gateway to the Dreamtime. This smoke is a healer; come, breathe it.'

The fire had been primed with fresh green branches. As it billowed with white aromatic smoke we were led slowly around it. Some of us wept cool tears, some of us simply smiled; we breathed deeply and allowed the smoke to penetrate our personal cuts and private wounds. Memories of Mary's handover came flooding back; I thought of my family, my parents, the elders with eyes full of forgiveness, and cool tears streamed down my cheeks. Gone was the psychiatrist's couch, gone were the 'If You Don't Like It, Leave' bumper stickers. As I drew the smoke into my being I felt a peace rise through the soles of my feet. Our procession snaked its way around the 'sacred flame' in a continuous circle, and all of us – black, white, country, city, rich and poor – became one.

{ 18 APRIL 2006 }

The first thing I saw when I opened my eyes the next morning was that portrait of David Gulpilil. Even on paper he dominated the room. I stretched out, feeling fresher and more alive than I had since those dark days over Christmas and New Year. I had tried phoning Gary a few times the previous evening and each time the phone rang out. I wasn't too concerned;

I was getting used to things unfolding naturally and in their own time. I knew we'd meet soon enough. After breakfast I phoned Jason, who boomed down the line, 'Hey! Welcome to Melbourne, my brother.'

I told him I was having trouble making contact with Gary. 'Phone me this afternoon, I'll sort everything out,' he promised. I headed into the city again; it was a long walk but the walking seemed to make me feel strong again, as if I was purging my system of all those life-robbing chemicals.

I arrived at the information desk of the Melbourne Museum and asked if Simon from the Indigenous Collection was in. Minutes later we were shaking hands. Simon led me to the Museum cafeteria. Over coffee, I told him all about Mary's return and of the positive effect that it had had on my family. He smiled as I recounted the driving incidents and laughter I'd shared with Bob and Jason.

'You were lucky with Mary,' he said. 'In the vast majority of cases we have no idea where the remains have come from. But we can't just hand them all over the way some clans want us to, that would be irresponsible; the Museum would have to answer to future generations if we did that.'

He went on, 'You know, Jason really burnt some bridges here, the museum had no choice but to let him go.'

'Well, I can understand his point of view,' I replied. 'He literally tripped over the remains of his ancestors, didn't he?'

Anger flashed across Simon's face before softening into sadness. 'The trouble with the clans is, they think they're the only ones allowed to feel. I'm up there in those storerooms day after day, is it so hard to imagine that I might speak to them too? When we're alone, I talk to them.' He looked away.

I told Simon that once enough water had passed under the bridge, that once I was strong enough, I might write a book about Mary's return to country. One story to speak for all the bones still in drawers and about the people on both sides of the fence who cared deeply about them. Simon looked at me intensely. 'I can't believe anyone would be interested in what I do up there, about the way I feel.'

'I reckon they would,' I answered. 'It's your side of the story that makes it complete.'

A friend of mine once commented that one of the stumbling blocks to Reconciliation in Australia is that too many people believe that all blackfellas are mystical and that all whitefellas are mean. And as Simon organised a special visitor's pass for me I understood fully what my friend had meant. 'Make sure you check out Bunjilaka,' he said, pointing me in the direction of the Museum's Indigenous collection. 'We're really proud of the work we've done there.' As he walked away he turned and called, 'And say hello to Mary for me!'

At the northern end of the museum, past the Cobb & Co Coaches and other pioneer displays, lay the entrance to Bunjilaka. As I entered the first section my heart literally jumped for joy. I'd walked straight into an extensive exhibit on possum-skin cloaks. All around me were stunning reproductions and new designs, the ancient tools of the craft as well as the new ones. I watched a video display featuring the ladies who were reviving and reinterpreting the craft. But best of all, there in a softly lit glass case was the Lake Condah cloak, one of only six nineteenth-century cloaks in existence (of which four are held in overseas collections).

After an hour I wandered into the next exhibit, which featured a display on Aboriginal burials and the importance of a final return to country. Central to the exhibit was a long black Chrysler hearse featuring

Aboriginal flags on the front doors. The hearse was purchased in 1976 by the Aboriginal Advancement League and made available for the return of Indigenous people to their own country for burial. I felt a strange connection to the hearse, and peering into its windows tried to imagine the drivers and their assistants who sat upon the broad bench seats as the wagon traversed the highways and dusty back roads of Victoria.

After spending half the day in the museum I headed for the exit, overloaded with new insights and understandings. A flash of red and black caught my eye. The museum gift shop had a display of cuddly toy birds in the window, and sitting among the many species displayed was my old friend, the Red-tailed Black Cockatoo. I purchased two birds for my daughters and as the sales assistant put them in my shopping bag she gave each of the cockatoos' tummies a playful squeeze, setting off the little soundbox inside. 'Karak! Karak!'

My legs took me south again, towards the Domain parklands and the 'sacred flame'. But the mood there was different this time. A television crew from one of the commercial stations' current affairs shows had set up on the perimeter. The male reporter, a large oaf in an expensive-looking suit, was goading a couple of the young male firekeepers. The cameras were poised to start rolling the instant there was action. Meanwhile the sound man was swinging his long microphone boom through the air over the heads of the frustrated protesters.

'Oh sorry, are we violating your sacred airspace?' jeered the reporter.

Another reporter, a young dolly-girl in a tight mini dress, giggled and cooed at her male colleague. Eventually one of the young Koori men broke ranks and crossed the perimeter. He stood inches from the reporter's mocking face and half pleaded, half demanded, that the crew leave them in peace.

'You fellas have no idea what this place means to us, you have no idea how much pain you are causing us.'

The reporter had been waiting for this; he motioned to a ring of empty beercans that one of the technicians had fished from a nearby rubbish bin and arranged in a rough circle around the crew.

'Listen, you little black cunt,' he snarled, 'can't you see you're intruding on *my* sacred ground.'

The crew, especially the female reporter, fell about

laughing. A cameraman thrust his camera in the young Koori's face, waiting for him to snap. Summoning up a super-human level of self-restraint the young man turned his back on the reporter and walked slowly back into camp.

'You gutless little black shit!' the reporter called, clearly frustrated that he'd been denied some sensational footage. 'I'll be waiting for you.'

But despite the heavy mood, the supporters kept coming: a couple of young surfers, a dreadlocked hippy, two German tourists. I introduced myself to a local Koori girl who turned out to be a reporter for the local Indigenous radio station. When she heard of the reason for my visit, she whisked me to a quiet spot under a tree and with one hand holding a microphone and another wiping away tears, recorded my story of Mary's return. But there would be no smoking ceremony that afternoon, not as long as the media jackals prowled the perimeter.

As the sun set I headed north again, stopping at a phone box to touch base again with Jason.

'Hey, John! It's all set, we'll meet you at the pub in Nicholson Street at seven tonight, it's directly across the road from the Melbourne Museum.'

I set the alarm and collapsed into my bed for a two-hour nap. All that walking, all that emotion had gotten on top of me. I felt as though I'd packed a week into one day – and it still wasn't over! My friend dropped me at the pub just before seven; it was a nice place, tastefully decorated and softly lit. Jason arrived soon after and welcomed me with his beautiful big smile and a bear-hug. He was working for the Melbourne Comedy Festival, which was in full swing, and was still heavily involved with all his cultural obligations. Here was a man operating in two worlds; he looked tired.

An hour later a short, stocky fellow in a smart leather trenchcoat and black stockman's hat came through the door. He nodded to the barman and dumped a heavy briefcase on the floor beneath our table. It was the first time Gary and I had met. Gary had the quick eyes and disarming charm of a wheeler-dealer; he immediately reminded me of an Aboriginal version of Arthur Daley, the lovable rogue from the television show *Minder*. We quickly warmed to each other and he seemed impressed when I mentioned my visits to the 'sacred flame'.

'Jeez, you don't muck about do you,' he laughed.

'Two days and already you've got your finger on the pulse.'

We talked about family, Mary's reburial, and politics. Later in the evening a couple of Jason and Gary's friends joined us. As the jugs of beer steadily emptied, the laughter from our table became louder and the language fruitier. Gary held court and every so often banged his fist on the table to make a point or boomed out the word 'Bullshit!'

I looked around the room a couple of times, expecting to see disapproving looks from the other patrons or from the publican. But no one batted an eyelid. This wasn't one of those hard Queensland pubs where Aboriginal people were only let in under sufferance or relegated to a fenced-in beer garden. Here, Gary and Jason could make as much noise as anyone else; it might as well have been Gary's private club.

Gary was a masterful communicator; he could tell a story and knew how to drop his voice to draw in his audience. At one point he was explaining to me what the Koori struggle was all about. He swept a hand slowly over the table. 'Imagine that this table top is Victoria. Not so long ago it used to be ours, all of it. They tried to genocide our people and our culture so we wouldn't be around to prick their memories. They dug up the remains of our people to try to deny our existence. This tabletop represents 270 000 square kilometres, and do you know how much we own now?' He dipped his pinkie finger into the head of his beer and ever so gently placed the smallest drop of moisture onto the wooden surface. The entire room was hushed, as if each patron had been drawn into Gary's story. 'Not even that much. Less than 6000 hectares.'

It was a strange feeling sitting in that pub, which looked across at the Museum.

To Gary and Jason the Museum might as well have been an Alcatraz, imprisoning the remains and cultural properties of their people. And looking at those imposing floodlit walls surrounded by an empty no-mans-land of concrete I could certainly see their point of view. I mentioned that I'd had coffee with Simon earlier in the day and again Gary exclaimed, 'Jeez, where *haven't* you been! Two days and you're all over this town like a rash.' Then his voice softened, 'He's all right, our Simon, it's his masters that need educating. It's not just our ancestral remains they've got, I was in an advisory board meeting one day and one of the directors mentioned they had five hundred thousand of our spears in storage – five hundred thousand!'

As my mind wrestled with the concept of 500 000 spears, I felt sorry for those involved in this tug-of-war. Everyone I'd come into contact with seemed damaged in some way by it.

'Why can't there be a neutral burial place for the unidentified remains?' I asked. 'Like the shrine for the Unknown Soldier?'

'There's been talk of it,' answered Gary, 'serious talk, but you know how long it can take our mob to agree on anything, especially when it comes to country.'

A side door opened and a Koori man in his thirties walked in.

'Ah, here's our driver for tomorrow, Jida!' announced Gary.

I'd heard Gary's nephew's name mentioned throughout the night, particularly when the conversation concerned dance and song. Jason had turned to me a couple of times and remarked, 'Wait till you meet Jida. His dancing is up there, no one can touch him.'

Jida may have been a deadly dancer, but he could talk too! And every word was solid, convincing and powerful. Jida had visions; for himself, for the land, for his people, for everybody! With a mother from the Dja Dja Wurrung in Victoria and a father from Yolngu Country in the far north, here was a man with a sweeping outlook. Jida had the blackest eyes I had ever seen; they drew me in deep, and as he spoke I could see fire. At one point I said to him, 'You know, Jida, I can't help but get the feeling I'm talking to a future Prime Minister.'

'Phhttt!' he spat. 'Don't insult me, I've got plans!'

We both roared with laughter, but I knew I was in the presence of a future leader. I also knew I had made a friend.

CHAPTER SEVENTEEN

{ 19 APRIL 2006 }

A compact four-wheel-drive rolled up outside my friend's house just after 5 a.m. Jida swung my overnight bag into the back of the Mitsubishi and we headed off through the early-morning streets of Melbourne.

'We're picking up Gary next?' I asked.

'Gary's not coming,' said Jida. 'I just spoke to him. He's crook, his gout's playing up again, can hardly walk.'

Jida laughed. 'It's good in a way, we won't have to listen to country music for the whole trip. Gary loves

George Straight; plays him over and over.'

The drive to Swan Hill was over 400 kilometres and Jida talked for most of them. And like last night, it was good talk, not the ego speaking. If Gary was the natural communicator in the clan, Jida was certainly the natural educator. I asked plenty of dumb questions which he answered with patience. Once or twice, early in the trip, I asked him something a little too personal, something too direct, and he'd say, 'Whoa, hang on brother, I can't answer that, I hardly know you.' But by the end of our 800-kilometre journey I felt I could ask him anything.

Every now and then Jida mentioned his father in Arnhem Land who'd met the Queen and leaders from all over the world. But it wasn't until Jida mentioned his father's work in the movie business that the penny dropped.

'You mean you're David Gulpilil's son!?' I asked, 'I thought you were a Murray.'

'I am, my name is Jida Murray-Gulpilil,' he explained. 'My traditional name is Wayiniarr Marndarr, which means Lightning Thunder.'

I sat in silence for a long time. So many coincidences – or were they? The universe seemed to be contracting into tighter and tighter circles with every step I had taken in this journey to get Mary home.

'You know that portrait of your father, the one that won the Archibald Prize,' I said, 'it's hanging over my bed in the house where I'm staying. Your father has literally been watching over me for the last three days.'

Jida simply nodded and smiled. He also understood the power of not saying anything; of silence.

We passed through many pretty towns, including the goldrush city of Bendigo, but it was the natural features that were of more interest to Jida.

'See that mountain over there?' he said pointing to the east. 'That's Pyramid Hill. Our people used to light signal fires up there which could be seen by the people as far away as Lake Boort.' Pointing to the west, he explained, 'That's almost one hundred kilometres away. They had a whole system of signals worked out; they could warn of danger, signal where the kangaroos were plentiful, invite neighbours to feasts, all sorts of things.'

As Jida explained the significance of each piece in the passing landscape, I began to see the country with new eyes. It was as if the European overlay was peeled away and I could feel the ageless, beating heart of the Earth. Wide open spaces were not empty voids; each part of the landscape had purpose and meaning. Jida explained all the things that had once been abundant in each area, and described the intricate trading routes that criss-crossed the country.

I realised that this man possessed a seemingly in-exhaustible source of knowledge. Indigenous history, sociology, creation stories, customs, song, dances; and not just from the south, but from the far north country of his father too. The sheer depth and potency of Jida's knowledge and understanding dwarfed anything a PhD doctorate could hope to offer. This was a learning that could only come through contact with the land and culture.

'We learn by listening, to Nature, to our elders,' he said. 'As a boy I travelled this road many times, taking our old ones home in my grandfather's hearse.'

'Not the one at the Museum!' I exclaimed as the universe turned in one more tightening circle. I remembered how I had peered into the hearse windows only the day before, and when no one was looking I had run my fingers along its shiny black paintwork.

'You know it!' said Jida happily. 'My grandfather was a great storyteller, but he was a trickster too. Once he stopped in a small town outside a milk bar. Two little boys were sitting outside and watched my grandfather go in; everyone knew the hearse, they knew his business. Then they watched him come out again with two ice blocks. He opened the back of the hearse and lifted the lid of the coffin slightly and handed one to the body, saying, "There you go, Uncle," then he opened his own ice block, winked at the boys and said, "Hot day, isn't it, lads?" before driving away.'

Jida laughed. 'Of course there was nobody in the back, but every time he drove through that little town the kids would run a mile.'

Somewhere around Lake Boga, Jida began to look periodically to the sky. I asked him what he was looking for.

'The Eagle; he's my bird, he welcomes me when I return to my country.'

Minutes later Jida pointed skyward. 'There, see him, he's always here to greet me!' Jida pulled off the road and drove down a little layby which ran to a creek. We got out and stretched, but this was more than a rest stop for Jida, he was home. He kneeled down and placed his palm upon the ground. Scooping up a handful of leaf litter, he squeezed it gently – not crushing it – and put it to his nose. I sat quietly on a log to let him get reacquainted with his country. He walked around, examining things I could not see. He placed a hand onto a tree trunk and called to me, 'This is my scar tree.'

As we passed Lake Boga and the land deteriorated, Jida's mood darkened. Whole expanses of countryside had been spoiled by salinity. I'd seen pictures of salt-ruined landscapes in books and on television, but nothing had prepared me for this. Whole paddocks were lifeless, poisoned, clapped-out.

We drove into Swan Hill, the bustling riverside town where my uncle – the one who had found Mary – once lived. Apart from the modern cars, it didn't look as though it had changed much in the 40 years since he had worked there as a veterinarian.

Jida had an inter-clan meeting to attend that evening so we wouldn't get to visit Mary's resting place until the next day.

'This place is really friendly,' said Jida, as we pulled into the forecourt of the Jane Eliza Motel. He wasn't kidding! The reception staff almost fell over themselves as they fussed over him. After dinner at the local RSL, he headed off to his meeting.

'Catch!' he called throwing me the keys to the car. 'Go for a spin, check out the town.'

I drove around the sleepy back streets of Swan Hill and wondered which neat little house my uncle and aunt had lived in. I followed the riverbank, past the lurid, gaping statue of the Murray Cod, and past the historic Pioneer Settlement that I had visited as a five-year-old. Within this re-created theme-park settlement, there sits a sundial dedicated to the pioneers who 'carved a nation out of nothing'. Heading north, I crossed the narrow bridge that spans the Murray and drove for a few kilometres; I was on Mary's side of the river now. As the sun dropped I pulled over on the deserted stretch of road. Jida had given me a CD of his traditional music, which included a song he'd composed for the recent reburial of Mary and his kin. I opened the car doors wide and sat on the roof listening to Mary's funeral song as it spilled from the speakers out into the purple Wamba Wamba dusk.

Yangurr waletya waletya aty
Werreka aty lar
Kayi kuthup
Yangurr waletya waletya aty
Ngaliyuk wawinpa kutnyuk
Werraka aty lar kumba
Nguteyuk kurruk pa yemin-yemin
Kayi kuthup kayi kuthup kayi kuthup

We come near you, approach you
To carry you home
I'm sorry
We come near you, approach you
Our brother and sister
To carry you home, to lie down and sleep
Your country and burial ground
I'm sorry, I'm sorry, I'm sorry

WARRPA WOY!

Reburial Song
Jida Gulpilil

{ 20 APRIL 2006 }

Mary is buried on Menera Station, a 1600-hectare property a few kilometres east of Swan Hill on the New South Wales side of the Murray. The property has seven kilometres of river frontage and cost the Wamba Wamba over two million dollars. The Wamba were also interested in the adjoining property when it came up for sale, but when the property owner discovered that the interested buyers were Indigenous people, the price suddenly doubled, putting it beyond their reach. Menera is traditional language for 'we're all friends'.

'Welcome to Menera, brother,' said Jida as he turned off the road and through the gates of the property. We drove down the long central farm road. Jida waved to a harvester in a distant paddock and the driver waved back. Properties of this size cost a lot to maintain and Menera is still a working enterprise, but the best land has been set aside as a cultural sanctuary, a place to conduct spiritual business and as a final resting place for Wamba Wamba ancestors. We pulled up at the shearers' quarters, a long, well-kept, corrugated-iron building. At one end was a basic kitchen and an adjoining room containing a few worn-out lounge chairs. The rest of the rooms contained beds, holding bare mattresses that looked almost as old as the Dreamtime. Jida took me to the last room and opened the door. 'This is where we housed the remains for a few weeks while we made preparations for the burial. Mary waited here before going back to Mother Earth.'

We continued across the property to the river and parked at the main house. The farmhouse was surrounded by a green lawn and rickety, vine-covered fence. The station manager was out. Looking for a suitable place to store the camping supplies and equipment he had brought up from Melbourne, Jida wandered in and out of machinery sheds and outbuildings. The smells of fertilisers and feed bags brought back memories of my childhood, when I followed my father into sheds just like these.

When Jida found the right spot he backed the car into a shed and unloaded his gear before carefully covering everything with an old canvas tarpaulin. 'I'll be back in a few weeks doing some cultural business, this is some of the gear I'll need,' he explained.

We wandered up onto the levee bank and sat watching the river slide past. An ancient aluminium houseboat, no bigger than the smallest caravan, sat tethered to the great root of a river red gum. A lone shirt dried in the still air and a fishing line ran limp into the water, but no one was home.

'Who lives there?' I asked.

'Can't remember his name,' answered Jida, 'but he's a good fella, a Vietnam veteran. Hardly leaves the river; spends all his time travelling up and down in his tinny pulling rubbish from the water. Collects garbagebags full.'

I followed Jida along the riverbank. A neighbouring farmer eyed us suspiciously from the far bank before Jida disarmed him with a wave and a smile. He walked though the scrubby bush easily, silently, while I crashed and crunched behind.

'We've got big plans for this place: ecotourism, bush tucker, an education and training centre for our young people.'

'See this dried-up billabong,' he said, pointing to a large patch of ground which to me looked just like a hollow. 'I want to pump water back into it and create a living water stage where we can put on night-time creation stories and concerts. It won't be like some fake Disneyland; I know how it can all be done so it blends in naturally. My family knows all the contacts to do it right: lighting people, sound people. I want people to come here and learn, so that when they go away they'll see the country the way we see it.'

As I looked about I could see it. And I believed that I'd one day return to see Jida's vision a reality.

We drove on through a desolate expanse of the property in silence. It was sparsely vegetated with stunted saltbush – not even weeds grew here. It reminded me of the badlands from a Western movie. Decades ago, some farmers along the Murray learnt that the 'camp ovens' or middens – some of which were up to two kilometres long – made inexpensive and fast-draining road surfaces. Entire middens, which often included burial sites, were excavated and turned into service roads. I wondered if we were driving over one of the infamous 'oven roads' now, across the ground-up bones of Mary and Jida's ancestors. Considering our destination, I thought it prudent not to ask. We parked at a dried-up creek crossing; across on the other side the land softened into green again.

'The burial site is on the other side,' Jida explained.

'We need to be smoked before we can cross over.'

As Jida built a ceremonial fire I looked around at the surrounding trees. They were ancient trees and in their gnarly knots and bark bunions I saw their spirit faces. These were the sentinels of the bridge and our observance of Law determined whether we would receive their benevolence or suffer their wrath. White smoke curled skywards and Jida came towards me with a smoking sapling. I stood with my arms outstretched, as if I was passing through an airport security gate. I let the smoke pat me down and remove bad spirits from my pockets, from my soul. The air began to vibrate against my skin, as if the atmosphere around us had changed to a higher, faster frequency.

'It's okay, we can cross now,' said Jida quietly.

We climbed into the car and drove across the wooden bridge. The faces on the trees were close, watching us as we passed. I felt their breath.

'Those trees had faces, did you see . . .'

Jida drove on slowly without answering.

As we rose up out of the dip the atmosphere returned to a more familiar frequency. I say 'frequency' because that is the only way I could describe it.

We drove to a gated fenceline and Jida announced

our arrival. Passing through the gate I stood before two rows of mounds. Beneath each one lay a Wamba Wamba man, woman or child. Jida walked to one of the mounds and said, 'I'm pretty sure that this one belongs to Mary. I put him in the ground, I remember because he really stood out.'

'Why, did you get a sense that it was him, did it feel different to the others?' I asked, expecting a mystical, otherworldly explanation.

'No, it was because he was bright yellow.'

I burst out laughing and when I explained the coats of lacquer that Dad had applied over the years, Jida laughed too. How was I expected to stay solemn now! Jida left me alone. I tried to feel profoundly moved, appropriately emotional. I removed my boots and socks and wiggled my toes into the red earth, trying to feel something more, some connection with my old friend, but I couldn't. Mary was back in the ground where he belonged and that was that.

I walked back to the car and placed my boots on the bonnet. Jida was nearby, scratching about in the faint remnants of a fire. With a stick he overturned old coals, revealing half-melted metal tags. The tags bore serial numbers. 'This is where we burnt the specimen boxes,' he explained. 'Our ancestors were all tagged with numbers; Mary was the only one with a name.' He pointed to a large patch of bare earth. 'We set the marquee up over there, that's where the guests sat. Koories from all over Victoria and New South Wales came to say goodbye. At the end everyone came forward and threw gum leaves into the open graves upon the bones.'

Jida led me to a large mound behind the burial site which he explained was a camp oven. I imagined it was just like the one my uncle had pulled Mary from, over 40 years ago. Rabbits had burrowed into its sides, displacing century-old clay balls used for cooking. As I gazed upon Wamba Wamba country from the top of that ancient mound, a clay ball in my hand, the feeling I'd had in the bush as a child returned. It felt as if the original occupants had been here only moments before. And in a sense that was true.

Jida walked towards the nearby billabong, and as I followed I walked into a clump of thistles. Falling to my backside I yanked the painful needles from my tender soles.

'What did you take your boots off for?' demanded Jida as I sat wincing on the ground.

'Well, don't you ever like to feel the soil under your feet?' I shot back.

'Not around here, I don't; I'm not silly, you know.'

We both broke up laughing again. I hobbled to the shady bank of the billabong and plonked down besides my friend. With my pocketknife I managed to scrape most of the thistles from my feet.

A couple of ducks glided by and I asked Jida if they were good to eat.

'Of course,' he said, 'You mean you've never had roast duck?'

'So how would you get them, with a spear or a shotgun?' I asked, thinking I'd covered all bases.

'Too hard with a spear, too messy with a shotgun. What I'd do is get into the water and gather up a whole bunch of reeds and sticks. Then with my face just sticking out of the water I'd gently, *gently*, float close by. Then when a duck swims by I'd just grab him by the legs and pull him under. No noise, no mess – easy! His duck brothers wouldn't even know what had happened to him.'

I nodded. 'That does sound like a good way to catch duck.'

We sat for a long time in silence, soaking in the spirit of the billabong.

'You know,' said Jida eventually, 'Mary's journey home is a story about love. I think I'll write a song about it.'

I didn't answer; the breeze that rippled across the water did that for me. And while I sat there with Jida under that clean Wamba Wamba sky, lazily watching those ducks that would live to swim another day, I can't say I felt healed. I just felt good. As though I belonged. As though I had come home.

AFTERWORD

I met John Danalis once in 2005, after he contacted me to ask if he could use a black cockatoo feather headdress he had seen on display during one of my talks at the Brisbane Writers Festival.

I will never forget the impact of those words, 'a skull on our mantelpiece'; he might as well have kicked me through my gut with the heel of his foot. But I immediately thought that if this whitefella was bold enough to first call me about the headdress, and then make an effort to turn up at my doorstep in pursuit of it, I should at least listen to what he had to say, and I mean really listen.

I knew it wasn't a decision that I had the right to make; my spirit belly knew that the decision had already been made by the Spirits, our old people. This was business that did not need my reaction, but my contribution.

I remember clearly and quite simply saying to Johnny, 'He or she needs to go home', and this story confirms to me over and over again that John Danalis got the message. We need to go home. To Country. At any point throughout time . . . we need to go home.

This story is the first yarn I know of told by a whitefella who appears to have entered into *our place*. He has begun to *connect*, to quite simply, *get it*. The journey is yet to unfold from here on now, but the connection process has begun, Johnny Danalis has begun to see things, this place, this country, the people, through the eyes of The Dreaming.

I can only imagine how strong the *heartbeat* and *Spirit face* of this Country would be if our collective eyes could begin to do the same.

{ FIONA DOYLE OOCHUNYUNG

CAIRNS, APRIL 2009 }